SightShift: Identity

5 Actions to Discover Freedom from Comparison and Fear

Chris McAlister

with Bret Burchard

Copyright © 2013 SightShift Publishing, LLC
1280 W 5th Ave, Suite 113
Columbus, OH 43212

Printed in the United States of America

ISBN: 098998530X
ISBN-13: 978-0989985307

Faith is: that the self in being itself and in willing to be itself is grounded transparently in God.

Soren Kierkegaard

CONTENTS

HOW TO READ THIS BOOK

The initial format I created for leading people through SightShift was in a retreat setting. Reflective assignments and introspective exercises are a core ingredient to helping others experience their true self.

Obviously, this is a book so that aspect is limited. Rather than fill the end of each chapter with introspective questions, I wanted readers to move from idea to idea.

So here's what I'd suggest instead: if you find an area that resonates with you or you'd like to revisit, dog-ear the page. Once finish the book, revisit those sections you've marked and journal, reflect and dive deeper.

SECTION 1

cooperate

1

A CONFUSED PROCESS

Sitting on my deck in the fall of 2008 with an eviction notice on the front door, I felt like I was scraping the bottom of my soul. I was barely making enough money to put gas in the car and struggling to feed my wife and daughters. I had hit rock bottom. There was nothing left in me. My relationships were fracturing, my work was suffering. I did not know who I was or what I was supposed to be doing. I was grasping for something to hold onto and searching for answers.

The way I filtered the events of my life was completely broken. What mattered most was how much I could get done and how happy people were with me. I have now learned to focus more on who I am becoming. I have learned that who I am shapes what I do and the quality of relationships I enjoy. I want to help you understand that who you are, your identity, is foundational, not your mission or community.

Identity > mission > community

Six years prior to receiving the eviction notice I went to work for my father's large church with the long-term goal of taking over leadership when he retired. Soon after joining the staff, my colleagues started looking to me for guidance. The intended 7-10 year plan for my dad to transition the church turned into a 2-3 year plan. I was on the fast track. We were broadcasting services on TV and radio, and had just completed a $15.3 million building project. It was everything a young, ambitious pastor could want.

As the timeline shortened, I realized some things were not going to change before the church and I engaged in the transition. I became unsettled with the idea of taking the reins of leadership. I did not like who I was becoming. In November 2006, just four years after joining the staff, I revealed this new perspective to my dad. It was not just a two-week notice to a boss who didn't care. Imagine telling your father, "Everything you have spent nearly two decades building, I don't want it." It was a difficult conversation, but I was trying to follow God and trust that He would take care of me.

A few months later, I was out. I had no job, no income and a wife and three daughters at home. I was so fried and burned out by church that I did not even attend a service for five months. My family celebrated Easter in our living room by dancing to a Toby Mac CD. I had no interest in going to church and little interest in being a pastor anymore. But I had a family to take care of and was trying to follow what God wanted me to do.

Through a connection I was offered an opportunity to explore leading a church in my wife's hometown. After some research and conversations with the staff, it appeared to me we were two different entities headed in two different directions. They had been in decline for about seven years and based on how I am wired, it was a dangerous combination. I had my reservations but I also felt pressure to provide for my family. The more I met with the church leaders, the more I became convinced of their desire to change and my ability to help them. I agreed to jump on board and took over with immense clarity, laying out a vision of 17 ways we were going to change. I thought I was approaching this new endeavor as a strong, focused leader. Turns out I was a scared, insecure one.

After a year into the transition we had made no progress. We tried everything but hit rock bottom financially. We sold the church van to pay electric bills and I was barely making enough money to drive to work on Sundays. Some people would have shut down in panic, but I became hyperactive. I tried everything I could think of to make some extra money and provide for my family. I considered coaching, counseling and even network marketing. I ended up substitute teaching, making about a third of what I needed to provide modest food and shelter for my wife and children.

Unfortunately, the financial needs of raising a family include more than just food and shelter. There was also the comfort of my late-night bowls of cereal. I skipped them. There was the street fair with the $5 Ferris wheel my daughter begged me to ride. I went to a pawnshop but only managed enough to buy tickets for two of my three kids. There was Christmas. My wife sold her engagement ring for presents.

We fell a couple months behind on our house payments. I thought I had arranged an agreement to catch up on them later when we had the money, but came home one Friday to an eviction notice on the front door. For the rest of the weekend my heart vacillated between peace and fear, wondering what to make of our circumstances.

I felt completely defeated. There was nothing left in me. I remember thinking to myself: "I do not know who I am. I do not know what I am supposed to do. I am a failure as a pastor. I am a failure as a provider. What if we are kicked out of our house? What if I lose everything? How am I defined? Who am I?"

Have you ever struggled with questions about who you are? Questions regarding your identity are the most foundational questions you will face. Your answers will affect every other part of your life. It will affect your passion, your calling, your response to success or failure, and your relationships.

Unbeknownst to me at the time, my primary ambition in deciding to receive the leadership baton from my father was to pastor a mega church. I wanted to stand in the sanctuary, look around and say, "I built this with my life!"

My primary motivation for taking over the second church was not to spark transformation, but to be the white knight and hero, saving it from devastation.

I have spent most of my life building my identity around mission. I need to perform well to feel worthy. Some people build their identity around community and certain relationships they feel they need. If you build your identity around anything that can be gained or lost, you are set up for crisis. There is only one thing you can build your identity around that cannot be gained or lost: God's love. Who you are, your identity, is created to be defined by His love.

When I was 16 years old and learning to drive a stick shift, my buddy Jerry and I went for pizza in my first car. It was a white, boxy Honda Civic. After leaving my house, the first stoplight we came to was on a hill and we were in the front of the line. I shifted into first gear, the light turned green and I stalled trying to accelerate. I couldn't go anywhere. I repeated the same misstep through two more light changes. I was stuck. Drivers behind me were becoming agitated. I was freaking out. Sixteen-year-old sweat glands were not built for this kind of pressure.

Then Jerry took over. He jerked up the emergency break, made me shift into first gear and told me to give it a little gas. I was so nervous that "a little gas" turned into "a lot of gas." When the light turned green Jerry dropped the break. Heavy-footed on the pedal, we screeched out of the hill off to the right and down the road.

There is finesse to driving a standard transmission. You can shift straight into second gear on a flat surface and get away with it, but when you are on a hill you have to know how to shift into first gear.

The same is true with our lives. Identity – who you are – is first gear. We have been trained to shift straight into second and third gears – mission and community. We are obsessed with our purpose and our relationships. When life is smooth and the journey is flat, we can get away with a heavy focus on second and third gears. On the hills of life, you have to learn how to shift into first gear: Identity.

I have devoured every piece of literature I could find on identity. I have been on a constant quest exploring identity in my own life and with others. I learned the hard way. I want to help you learn who you are before you hit an existential crisis. I want to help you learn how to shift into first gear on the hills of life before crisis overwhelms you.

Some of you will still go through the crisis. Some, as we see in biblical characters, have to go through the crisis to have a sense of awakening. It will play out differently for different people, but there is a perfect example of identity development in scripture. I want to help you learn how to cooperate with that process. The example is Jesus.

Each of us carries assumptions about Jesus that have damaged our ability to relate to Him and participate with the development that God has for us. I want to help you rediscover what is true about you and Him.

A secure identity overflows into clarity in mission, which builds and attracts healthy community. It all starts in first gear with a clear understanding of identity.

2

A CLEAR PROCESS

When we fail to appreciate that Jesus came to restore humanity, we strip the incarnation of its power. For Jesus, being fully human was to live a life submitted to the Father and empowered by the Spirit. He is our example of true humanity in its fullness, life in relationship with God and others.

Church history has affirmed that Jesus was both fully God and fully man. Scripture also tells us in Philippians 2 that Jesus emptied Himself. He did not give up being God. He gave up access to the power He had as God in order to grow as we grow. The Gospels show us that He physically grew as we grow, and He intellectually and emotionally grew as we grow. We grow and develop in our self-awareness. We take for granted what it was like for Jesus to also grow and develop in His identity or self-awareness.

We know from scripture that Jesus struggled in every way we struggle. He never sinned, but He did face our same struggles. He faced cultural pressures, He faced social pressures, and He even faced internal questions about His identity.

At some unknown moment in Jesus' development as a human being He realized, "I am the Son of God." There is no biblical evidence that tells us the one-year-old Jesus laid on a bed and thought, "You better change my diaper. I'm the Son of God. I'm kind of a big deal." We have no evidence that at age four He was comfortable sharing toys because He knew He could just make more out of nothing. At some point while being raised in the Jewish culture, maybe Jesus read about the suffering servant of Isaiah and realized, "This is me. I must suffer and die to redeem the world."

We do not know exactly the moment Jesus grasped His identity as the Messiah, but we do have strong biblical data to walk us through the process the Father used to develop the Son as His path emerged.

We start with the baptism of Jesus in the Gospel of Luke.

When all the people were being baptized, Jesus was baptized too. And as he was praying, heaven was opened and the Holy Spirit descended on him in bodily form like a dove. And a voice came from heaven: "You are my Son, whom I love; with you I am well pleased." Luke 3:21-22

In this moment, Jesus received affirmation from the Father. It was not a performance-based statement. This was not a calling to suffer and die for the world. This moment was not the Father celebrating the Son's performance. He was celebrating the Son's personhood.

The Father expressed delight in the Son before the Son did anything. Personally, as a father, I would have mishandled this moment by celebrating the extreme performance of what was coming on the cross. Yet, the Father, as a perfect parent, celebrated personhood over performance. Jesus had not begun His ministry and the Father said, "I am pleased with you." The Father affirmed His love for the Son for who He was, no strings attached.

This was the affirmation of identity. After this affirmation, Jesus was led into the wilderness by the Spirit where He faced temptation. Before Jesus could deliver Israel in a communal way, He had to first face the devil in a personal way. He does that in Luke 4.

In verse three, the devil tempts Jesus by challenging Him. "If you are the Son of God…"

Jesus had just been told at the baptism: "You are the son." Now the enemy is challenging Him. "*If* you are the Son…"

Every moment of your life can be defined by what the Father wants to make real to you concerning your identity. The enemy wants to convince you it is a conditional reality. We become so obsessed with second gear (mission and calling) and third gear (community and relationships) that we miss the unconditional reality of first gear (identity). In this passage in Luke, Jesus experienced an attack on first gear, His identity. He was targeted directly where the Father just spoke to Him.

The specific temptation in Luke 4:3 is significant. "The devil said to him, 'If you are the Son of God, tell this stone to become bread.' "

Based on my research, there are two interpretations regarding this text throughout the history of the church[1]. One interpretation is on a surface level, acknowledging that Jesus was being tempted to provide for himself. He faced a test similar to the test Adam faced in the Garden of Eden. Would Jesus trust His Father, or like Adam, would Jesus decide God's provision was not enough? We discover in this account that Jesus was the perfect Adam. Where Adam fell, Jesus did not.

There is also a second, deeper meaning. The Jewish reader would have connected the dots. Moses, through miracles, led the children of Israel into a space where God provided for them. Jesus, by launching out as the Messiah, believed He was the new and true Moses, come to set the people free, come to lead them out. And that is where the enemy attacked Jesus: "If you are the new and true Moses, prove it by what you do. Tell the stone to become bread." He did this twice, challenging Jesus to prove who He said He was: "If you are the Son of God…"

The dialog here is so profound, so life changing, and is the vital clue to what is happening in your life at any given moment. There is a constant temptation. The enemy wants you to define who you are by what you do or who you are in relationship with. The Father wants to repeatedly take you back to the truth: You are not defined by what you do. You are defined by who the Father says you are.

Your daily existence is a tension between the Father wanting to build your identity and the enemy wanting to threaten it. Jesus responded to this by passively receiving the affirmation of who He was from the Father and then actively rejecting the accusation of the enemy. Receive who you are. Reject who you are not. Then you will, like Jesus, emerge with clarity in mission.

Coming out from the wilderness, Jesus went into the synagogue. During the time for reading from the scrolls, Jesus stood in front of the religious leaders and crowd as He read from Isaiah:

> *"The Spirit of the Lord is on me, because he has anointed me to preach good news to the poor. He has sent me to proclaim freedom for the prisoners and recovery of sight for the blind, to set the oppressed free, to proclaim the year of the Lord's favor."* Luke 4:18-19

Before Jesus emerged with clarity in mission, He first endured the testing of who He was. He went through the testing of His identity (You are my Son) then overflowed clarity in mission (this is what I must do). Then we look to Luke 5 and the calling of the first disciples. In verse 10 Jesus says to Simon, "Don't be afraid; from now on you will fish for people." With the mission clear, Jesus attracted and built community.

This is the process the Father used to build the Son. Jesus' identity was affirmed. He moved into second gear, clarity in mission. Then He moved into third gear, building a healthy community to accomplish that mission. This is the process the Father is using to conform you to the image of the Son.

We feel pressure to figure out what we should do with our lives, what our purpose or calling is, and what kind of relationships we should have. The Father wants to continually remind us of who we are. He wants to give us ownership and empowerment to live out a clear mission. As a clear mission overflows out of who we are, we will attract and build healthy community.

Scripture teaches us that we are not to remain stuck in an infantile dependency on God, nor should we live independently from God. There is a tension of needing Him for our identity but at the same time learning to grow in our empowerment to make choices in our mission and community. We find over and over in scripture that while we are obsessed with second and third gears, God keeps inviting us back to first gear, identity.

We will explore how to learn who you are by discerning where your identity is threatened. When you learn where the enemy is seeking to sell a lie about who you are then you can flip it and recognize where God wants to build you. I have learned that the center of the enemy's attack on my heart is I am not worthy unless I perform well. God wants to

Chris McAlister

continually help me see, feel and hear that I am worthy regardless of performance.

The more you know who you are, the more clarity you will have to pursue mission. If you are clear in mission, you will attract people. They will want to be on mission with you and in relationship with you, and a community built on a secure identity will be healthy.

While this process is sequential, mission and community can reinforce who we are as long as they are not the primary place from which we derive our identity. The process is identity first. This is the process the Father used to build the Son and the one He is using to build your life. A secure identity overflows to clarity in mission, which attracts and builds healthy community.

If you are not aware of the process then you will be like many who live frustrated lives rather than cooperate with the Father's process. You will beg God to show up in your mission or your relationships. That is not how the Father works. He is constantly speaking to our identity first.

This is the rhythm and flow of Jesus' life. He modeled for us God's will, to be submitted to the Father and empowered by the Spirit. Now, we are to be conformed to the image of the Son.

He wants to help you receive your identity. It will overflow into clear mission. And you will attract and build a healthy community.

3

IDENTITY IS FOUNDATION

Identity is how you see yourself or how you experience yourself. More than just your thoughts, it is your internalized image of yourself. It is where you find affirmation, meaning and validation[2].

You want to feel peace about who you are. You want to know who you are. You get to choose what or whom you build your identity around, but know this, your brain can work against you. Your brain wants a story of who you are that makes sense. When a man beats on you, it is easier for your brain to falsely believe it is your fault. When a religious leader shames you, it is easier to falsely believe you don't measure up. We believe lies about ourselves regarding our identity because our brain forced a false story. We ignore what does not add up.

Our brains will choose a negative, shame-based identity if it is an easier ideal to live up to than the positive identity we feel like we cannot attain. We will naturally choose the path of least resistance. We will make God out to be a Zeus and choose a rebellious identity connected to defiance. Or like many I have observed in Christianity, we will choose an identity based on subservience. Unhealthy cultures emphasize servanthood over God's intended primary identity for us: child. Humanity's chief qualifier for its identity is not rebels or servants but sons and daughters.

For me, in 2008, when the church was in decline and our family hit rock bottom, I chose the negative, shame-based identity that I was a failure. I took the position as pastor to be the knight in shining armor and the situation only got worse. My brain forced a false story that if I had been a better leader I would have been able to take care of my family.

Jesus, as the true alternative, modeled cooperation with the process the Father uses to grow us. We receive who we are from the Father. This true identity from the Father will be tested in the wilderness. As we emerge from the wilderness we will find clarity in what we are to do. That clarity will help us build and attract healthy relationships.

Sometimes those wilderness periods are short. Sometimes they are long. Sometimes they are simply moments throughout our day when we feel vulnerable. When Jesus went off alone to pray He went back to solitude and surrendered the temptation to build His identity around anything false. He needed to be reminded that He was who the Father said He was.

If you build your identity around anything that can be gained or lost, you are setting yourself up for a crisis.

Yet a challenge remains. The shaping of your identity is dynamic, not static. You could build your identity around any role, possession, achievement or relationship that comes along. Just because you learn how to reject the accusations of the enemy and build your identity around who the Father says you are does not mean your identity is a fixed staple of your life. It is a constant process of surrendering. You will still face hardships and in those moments you will navigate them either through a secure identity built around who the Father says you are, or a false identity built around something else. In my life, I have noticed an increasing awareness of the temptation to build my identity around something false. I am learning to recognize through the

Spirit's influence when I have lost my true center and how to quickly return.

Jesus wants to help walk us into the family of God so that we know at all times who we are, even when we feel weak and threatened. Jesus, the Great Shepherd, knows where our true home is. He knows how to walk you home with Him and He is your home every time you need Him to be. God created us for secure attachment and we can only get what we need, the affirmation, meaning and validation, through an attachment to Him.

Jesus is our supreme example of a secure identity. He is our entryway into life with a good Father, shepherding Son and empowering Spirit. Life with God defines who we are.

4

THE CHIEF STORY ARC OF THE BIBLE

It is staggering that this identity-first concept is not emphasized consistently and explicitly in Christianity. Identity is the chief story arc of the Bible. We see it everywhere. Let's look at a few examples, beginning with one of the key patriarchs, Jacob.

Jacob

Jacob is a thriving businessman, having accumulated wealth, livestock and a huge family with two wives and children. About to face a brother he cheated, Jacob fears for his life. He panics, sending ahead gifts to buy his brother off and spare his life. He is a deceiver lost in second gear (mission) and third gear (community).

Mission and community are gone. He is alone. In this moment, he meets God face-to-face. They wrestle at the riverbank and God gives Jacob a blessing by changing his name. By addressing Jacob's name, God invites Jacob to be honest about who he is. He is Jacob, the deceiver. But God tells Jacob that he is no longer to be known as Jacob, a deceiver, but Israel, a prince. He is telling Jacob that he is not defined by what he does not have. He is defined by his relationship with God.

This is where the shift happens for Jacob. He learns to see God differently and he learns to see himself differently. You can learn to consistently partner with God, to shift into first gear, and to see who you are and who God is in truth. Just as He did with Jacob, God will invite you to be honest regarding what you build your identity around and He will speak a blessing to you. That blessing is a word spoken to you regarding who you are.

Moses

Moses dove into second gear first. In Exodus 2 he encounters an Egyptian beating a Hebrew brother. Feeling protective of his people, Moses steps in and kills the Egyptian. The next day he comes across two Hebrew brothers fighting and he again steps in to stop it. The Hebrews call out Moses, asking if he is going to kill them like he killed the Egyptian. Realizing what he did had become known, Moses flees, running into the wilderness in shame. For 40 years in the wilderness Moses takes care of his father-in-law's sheep. Imagine how Moses feels about himself at this point. For 40 years he tends to sheep; his father-in-law's sheep.

In this wilderness, Moses experiences God in an unexpected way at the burning bush. Here he is given his mission. He is to lead the Israelites out of oppression in Egypt. Moses thought he was ready for second gear long before when he protected the Hebrew from the Egyptian but he wasn't. He had to learn first gear first.

Through conversation, God invites Moses into this struggle of mission and identity, and this time Moses learns what is foundational. Moses asks God, "Suppose I go to the Israelites and say to them, 'The God of your fathers has sent me to you,' and they ask me, 'What is his name?' Then what shall I tell them?" (Exodus 3:13)

God responds, "...This is what you are to say to the Israelites: 'I AM has sent me to you.' " (Exodus 3:14)

God is defining first gear for Moses. He is telling Moses that what defines him is, "I AM is with you." From there he can move into second gear, leading the people out. Then together they will build a whole new community based on what it means to be in relationship to God.

By claiming to be I AM, God revealed He is the only being that does not need another qualifier to define his existence. God has always been. God is. God always will be. God is complete and whole within God. You need a qualifier to define your existence. I need a qualifier to define my existence. We get to choose what defines our identity.

Elijah

Elijah presents an example of someone who sees the apex of what a person hopes to see in his or her life. It is the big win, the top promotion, the closing of a deal or the crowning achievement. For Elijah, it involves ministry.

He is on the mountain facing 450 prophets of Baal by himself, standing up for God. He challenges the prophets to put their gods to the test. For the challenge, Elijah and the prophets of Baal each cut a bull into pieces and place it on the wood. Whichever god answers with fire, he will be acknowledged as the true God. The prophets of Baal dance and shout and slash themselves, calling on Baal to respond.

As their efforts fail, Elijah taunts them and mocks them to shout louder and try harder.

Then it is Elijah's turn. Almost arrogantly, he douses the altar with 12 large jars of water and prays to the Lord. God shows up in one of the mightiest ways we see in scripture. He sends down fire on the altar that consumes the sacrifice, the wood, the stones, the soil and even the water in the trench. Everyone around concedes that the Lord is God.

Can you imagine how cranked Elijah is? It was a huge victory, like winning the championship or being awarded the top prize in your field. Whatever that may be for you in your life, this is the mountaintop for Elijah. He had reached the pinnacle.

But what follows for Elijah is depression. He originally thought if God would show up on the mountain then all of Israel would turn and follow Him, but God did show up and all of Israel did not turn. Elijah becomes bitter and sad and is ready to quit. He dismisses his servant and retreats to the wilderness. God invites Elijah into the cave and they meet face to face.

God commands Elijah to stand in the presence of the Lord and sends down a powerful wind, an earthquake and fire. After the wind, earthquake and fire pass, Elijah hears the voice of God in a gentle whisper. Elijah experiences the truth that God is first found in first gear (identity).

To get to this point of maturity, Elijah had to endure a mission that did not go like he thought it should. He had a vision of a God who was only active in second and third gear. In the cave, his vision was corrected when he heard the still small voice.

Many people will hit rock bottom and think life is over, but what they don't realize is they are about to go into a new phase of mission in their lives. Learn that God is in first gear first. He is the still small voice that speaks to you and affirms your true identity.

Disciples

In Luke 10, Jesus sends out 72 men throughout the region to heal the sick. When they return to Him they are ecstatic about the success of their work, celebrating that even the demons submit to them. Jesus responds to their elation saying, "…do not rejoice that the spirits submit to you, but rejoice that your names are written in heaven." (Luke 10:20) Jesus is reminding them not to build their identity around mission, but around who they are.

The disciples were under the influence of adrenaline. Perhaps you can relate to that feeling after a big win.

Throughout my 20s I lived on the high of adrenaline. I was addicted. When the mission faded and community felt desolate there was no more adrenaline to fuel me.

Jesus Washing Disciples Feet

At the height of Jesus' ministry He stooped down and washed His disciples' feet. In the culture of biblical times the servant of the house would wash the master's feet. This was a monumental act of humility coming from the Lord of Lords and a demonstration of His propensity to serve others. This passage is taught as a command for us to follow His example and go serve. The problem with that approach is it becomes pressure to launch into second and third gear. In our haste to get to John 13:5, we dismiss John 13:3, which says, "Jesus knew that the Father had put all things under his power, and that he had come from God and was returning to God…" We bypass first gear.

Washing His disciples' feet was an overflow from Jesus' identity. He knew who He was in relationship to the Father (first gear), then shifted into mission to wash the disciples' feet (second gear). As the cycle continued, He built their community through the Last Supper (third gear).

When you receive the love and affirmation from the Father in first gear, you cannot help but overflow that to others. It may be through a physical act or it may be through a spoken word, or maybe through some other gift or act of service. When your identity is built around Jesus you can overflow the mission you are to accomplish, not the one you are pressured to accomplish.

There will always be good causes and compassionate things for you to do. You cannot do them all. Causes will move in and out of popularity as they consume the interest of the body of Christ with different emphasis, but you do not have to get swept up in the fads. Learn who you are and let that overflow to your mission.

Paul's Letters

Paul's letters in the New Testament are another example of how we like to bypass first gear and move straight into second and third gear. When we open up the letters we immediately pull out behavioral commands concerning how we should live and communal commands concerning how our relationships should operate. Those commands are in there, but they are a part of second and third gear.

Paul's pattern in the New Testament letters is to anchor you in first gear (identity) before flowing into how you live your life (second gear) and build your relationships (third gear). Whether he does it in a single sentence or half the book, his usual pattern is to first frame who we are in relation to God. For example, Ephesians chapters one through three are about who we are and who God is. Chapters four through six are about our mission and relationships. We work against the pattern God uses when we tell people what to do before they know who they are.

When our family moved to Columbus, Ohio, we had trouble selling our house. We tried everything we could think of, and finally I locked myself in the closet. I was going to stay there, fasting and praying until the house sold. I lasted a day. It didn't sell. We foreclosed.

I was putting God to the test in second gear. I challenged Him to act like I thought He should act in mission, or else He didn't really love me. But He does love me, and He gave me a gift that day. He showed me that my vision of Him was wrapped solely in how He responded to me in second gear. Over time I realized that it had more to do with my identity than anything else. I could still be secure and whole in who I am even though we had a house that foreclosed.

You already have a secure identity. It was given to you as a gift of your salvation. Now you can learn how to cooperate with the process the Father uses to build you and continually live that out. God wants to put a new filter on your life and help you learn how to shift into first gear. This is your opportunity to learn how to cooperate with that process.

SECTION 2

aware

5

SHAME IS THE PAIN

The key to learning how to cooperate with the process God is using to build your life is to first recognize what needs to be cleaned up. There is deconstruction before reconstruction. The deconstruction is the cleaning out of the junk or lies we have accumulated. Over time we hoard lies that block who we are. Freedom begins with unlearning those lies.

There is a reality television show that examines the lifestyles of people who use their place of dwelling to hoard. Clothes and trash pile up. Narrow passageways form. Living habits are altered because an unhealthy environment has developed. Waste multiplies and provides a home for maggots. The bugs are unavoidable. Imagine if the first solution to rid the bugs was to call an exterminator. It would sound ridiculous. One look at the place and anyone would notice that if they clean out the junk, the bugs would have no way to manifest themselves.

The same can be said for your identity. A healthy understanding of who you are is at the core of clarity in your mission and building healthy relationships. Surface-level answers and cheap remedies that overlook the struggle for identity are everywhere. They address the bugs but not the junk that attracts the bugs.

Struggling with porn? The cheap remedy is to get rid of your computer. That is bug management.

Worried about your finances? Make sure you give to your church. Bug management.

Wondering if your life has meaning? Serve to relieve the guilt. Bug management.

Suffocating in despair? Suppress what you feel. Bug management.

Bug management strategies can provide momentary relief but they fail to address the lies that attract the bugs. They deal with the fruit, not the root. So the same bugs or even different bugs will come back later. What is the real issue blocking your identity from being fully revealed?

At the root of our struggles with identity is shame. Shame is the junk that creates a breeding ground for the infestations. Shame has defined who you are. It is feeling that you are not going to have what you need, that you are an imposter, that you don't measure up and you are going to be found out.

To grasp shame's impact on you, look at the origin of humanity in Genesis 2 and 3. Adam and Eve have everything they need in the Garden of Eden and are perfectly taken care of. They do not have to be afraid of not measuring up or being found out. They are living in intimate relationship with God (identity), they are caring for creation (mission) and they are living in intimate relationship with each other (community). Humanity is created in God's Trinitarian image to live our identity, mission and community.

Yet everything changes when Adam and Eve go elsewhere to get what they need rather than going to God. They are sold a lie when the serpent says to the woman about eating from the tree, "You will not certainly die," the serpent said to the woman. "For God knows that when you eat from it your eyes will be opened, and you will be like God, knowing good and evil." Genesis 3:4-5

It was a lie because they already were like God. They had relationship with Him, they had mission and purpose, and they had intimate, vulnerable relationship with each other. They were already like God.

The enemy's selling point was they were missing out, that there was something more they could have, that God was holding out on them. The serpent convinced them they were not like God yet, but they could be. This is what we find at the core of sin in doubting God's goodness. Will God provide what we need or do we have to get it for ourselves?

At the height of human existence as it is recorded in Genesis, the people were naked and felt no shame. (Genesis 2:25) They were physically naked, yes, but even more they were in an exposed state of being. It is in this place where you are completely vulnerable yet know you are loved, you are accepted, you belong, you are taken care of, you will get what you need and you feel no shame.

After Adam and Eve take the enemy's bait, shame enters. They immediately run and hide. While hiding they make fig leaves to externally cover themselves and internally comfort their shame. Fig leaves are our attempt to control the overwhelming infestation and distract from the trash. A fig leaf is driving your 10-year-old to peak in baseball because you feel inadequate at work. Hyper-focusing on your son's batting average has more to do with your insecurity than your son's improvement. It is an external obsession to cover up internal shame. A fig leaf is a perfect lawn because you cannot understand or control your angry outbursts. It is bragging about your marriage when you really feel alone in the bed you share. A fig leaf is building your life plan to distract from the abandonment you felt when your parents divorced or scheduling plenty of nights out with friends to bury the terror of never feeling at home. A fig leaf is overworking to run from the fear that you will never be enough.

This is how shame manifests itself in our lives. When we feel shame we run and hide. We power up to prove something we do not truly believe about ourselves or we resign to believe a lie. We are afraid of the nakedness of who we really are so we run, hide and make fig leaves to cover up.

Yet when Adam and Eve run and hide, God seeks them out. God already knows where they are but He still asks them, "Where are you?" It is not an interrogating question laced with anger. It is not accusatory or said with vengeance. God's desire is for them to honestly face where they are.

They run off like scared, shamed children, but God comes to them with gentleness like a perfect Father.

Think about the kids who spend the afternoon creating un-commissioned artwork on the walls of their bedroom. If they hear dad's footsteps coming up the stairs their first reaction will be to run and hide. It is shame making them believe they need to cover up. But our good and perfect heavenly Father does exactly what we need Him to do. He does not approach Adam and Eve out of anger and punishment. He approaches in gentleness and love.

Hiding did not heal Adam and Eve's shame. Hiding will not heal your shame. In fact, shame gave them energy to hide, which is why you cannot evaluate your life based on energy. Shame can energize you and drive you to accomplish a lot, but evaluate your motives. You are not left alone in figuring out your motives. God knows you will be distracted by bugs and fig leaves so He calls you to face the junk or shame.

God comes to rescue Adam and Eve out of their shame. There is no rescue without facing reality. God asks the man why he is hiding. What is Adam's first response? He blames it on the woman God gave him. Then God turns to Eve. What is her first response? She blames it on the serpent. Whenever blame is at work it is birthed out of a person suffocating in shame. It comes from people who under the surface wonder if they belong, if they have what it takes, if they fit into the world, if they are going to be taken care of and whether or not their needs are a problem. Shame always wonders, who am I and where is home?

Understanding shame is key to understanding the biblical story. If you read through the Bible with a clear understanding of shame you will read it in a holistic way. The pervasive worldview of the biblical writers was shaped by shame and honor. The Western mindset is focused on guilt. Forgiveness of sins is a part of the story but it is not the whole biblical story. Forgiveness of sins is a restoration, a welcoming back, but ultimately forgiveness is for the healing of shame through a new identity in Jesus.

For example, when Jesus announced His mission, surprisingly, there is not one mention of forgiveness of sins. Yet Jesus infuriated religious leaders by offering forgiveness. Yes, forgiveness cleanses our self-righteousness, but we also need relief from our self-hate. We need to be delivered from the accusations of the enemy to know who we are in Jesus. What Jesus announced in His mission is what we receive: restoration into who we are.

Imagine if Moses approached the Israelites and said, "God knows you are enslaved in Egypt, He sees your troubles and wants you to know that He forgives you." The Israelites would wonder what they were being forgiven of and what they had done to deserve slavery. They still needed to see the blood on the door frame as a picture of forgiveness that is part of the story, but the bigger picture was a restoration of identity.

In our obsession with guilt we have missed the bigger, deeper reality of shame. Guilt is a part of the story, but shame is central. When you make a mistake it is good for you to know that you are forgiven, but more importantly you need to experientially know that you as a person are not a mistake. Guilt communicates you did something bad. Shame communicates you are bad. We must distinguish between the two.

When we read the story of Adam and Eve the chief filter for evaluating the human condition is the absence or presence of shame. Due to the Fall, humanity is broken. We have a proclivity to run and hide. We feel we do not belong, we are not enough, we do not have a place to call home. And that manifests itself in our lives as fear. Shame in who you are is the root of sin and it overflows to fear. We are afraid to be rejected and abandoned by God. Some writers in the Western church tradition claim that pride is the root of sin, but if you think about the most prideful people, it is not pride that is the root of their sin. They are insecure and afraid. I have never met a secure narcissist. Pride is not the issue. Shame is the issue and is central to understanding how God builds our identity.

How did and does Jesus help us with shame? He defeated and He defeats the shame.

Jesus was crucified outside of the city naked. He faced exclusion so we could be included. He was crucified naked as a symbol to restore what was lost in the Garden of Eden. Genesis records Adam and Eve's naked-and-feeling-no-shame as the height of human existence. Adam and Eve went from naked with no shame to losing who they are and hiding in shame. Jesus was crucified naked and suffered a death that was designed to shame. He faced the shame, despised the shame and by embracing the cross, He embraced the shame. Jesus died in the place of your shame.

Jesus struggled with a false view of God in His last moments on the cross like Adam and Eve did when they hid in fear. Adam and Eve falsely imagined a vengeful God out to get them because they had made a mistake. They were afraid He would abandon them. God had not changed. Adam and Eve's perception of God changed. Similarly, on the cross, Jesus lamented, "My God, my God, why have you forsaken me?" (Matthew 27:46) But the cross was an act of the Trinity. The Father gave the Son, the Son gave himself and the Spirit empowered the giving. At no point did the Father abandon the Son. When Jesus lamented His felt abandonment, He quoted Psalm 22. Reading Psalm 22 in its entirety, you find the psalmist felt abandoned but was not. Jesus willingly subjected Himself to suffer the cross to pay the price for our sins. Part of the price was feeling forsaken. Jesus felt forsaken so humanity can be delivered from feeling forsaken and know God in truth. Jesus felt the same despair as Adam and Eve, the perception that falsely imagined God had abandoned them. Shame breeds infestations because it distorts our image of God, which distorts our image of self.

Yet through the resurrection shame was defeated! The Son rose and was invited to sit at the right hand of God. In the culture of biblical times the right hand at the banquet was the seat of honor where there is no shame. The resurrection was the reversal of shame, and Jesus invites us into His life where shame loses its power to suffocate, deteriorate and diminish who we are.

If you are a Christian your identity in Christ is shame-free. Jesus said to his followers, "I am the way, the truth and the life." It was not an aggressive statement to prove who He was. It was an invitation to the only place that we can get what we need for our identity. We need a secure source to heal our shame and protect us from future shame. Adam and Eve had the Garden of Eden. They had everything they needed. You are invited back into that life where you know who you are, where you have a mission and a purpose that overflows out of your identity and where you engage in healthy relationships without shame.

6

FEAR IS THE MANIFESTATION OF PAIN

Your identity is shaped by the lie you believe about who you are. That lie is shame-based and manifests as fear. These fears are the chief way the enemy seeks to hurt us. Identity is a complex process, but the quickest way to figure out how God is building you is to look where the enemy wants to hurt you. The devil is a terrible poker player and he will show you where God wants to build you by the way he attacks your heart through lies. We are afraid because we have been hurt.

There are nine core fears[3] that will reveal with explicit clarity how the enemy wants to inflict pain and get you to believe a lie about God and yourself. You will see parts of yourself in each of these, but try to recognize the dominant one. That is where you will experience the most transformation. A look in the mirror can be painful. Life is on the other side, but the way through is deeper into the pain.

Fear 1: "If I'm not needed, then I'm not loved."

You live in such a way that people entangle themselves to you so that they need you. That is your fig leaf, how you cover the shame of being someone who is not loved. You position yourself and your relationships so that others need you. It is how you survive and how you go after life. If you are not needed then you do not feel loved. You have said yes so many times you feel like you don't know who you are anymore.

Fear 2: "If I don't take care of myself, no one else will."

You believe the only way you can feel some sense of joy in life is to be perfectly taken care of. The problem is it never happens. We were designed for perfect caretaking but we never get it from any human relationship. Once you realize you will not get the perfect caretaking you desire, you turn to escapism. That is your fig leaf. There is terror in your heart that you are going to be abandoned so you attempt escaping through destructive behaviors. This is masking the shame. You are trying to find relief but the quick relief from binging on destructive behavior numbs out your capacity to experience joy.

Fear 3: "I don't belong anywhere."

What is home for you? What is the place where everyone knows your name, the place you connect in a way you know you belong? You probably don't believe that place exists. You feel like you don't have a place to tie down into. You are so desperately trying to achieve peace in life through a sense of belonging that you ignore reality. You construct a fig leaf by kicking your problems farther down the road because you believe peace will come when there are no more problems. But there are always problems. None of us is ever problem free. True peace is an internal reality that empowers us to face external problems.

Fear 4: "I don't have what it takes."

Somewhere along the way you started to believe a lie that you don't have what it takes to get the job done. Maybe you were helping your dad work on the car and he lost patience with you, pushed you out of the way and took over, reinforcing the lie. Maybe your mom obsessed over your appearance, afraid you would die lonely. These moments made an entrance at some point in your life and sold a lie to your soul. You believe it in other areas of your life too, every area except one and you excel in that one area. You pour everything you have into that one thing so no one can ever again say that you don't have what it takes. You have specialized so much that you have trouble moving in and out of different roles. Maybe you have trouble relating at home. Maybe you are an excellent task master in your job but don't work well with others. Shame is screaming you don't have what it takes and you cover it up with the fig leaf of hyper-specialization.

Fear 5: "I can't perform well enough to feel worthy."

You believe you can only feel alive and worthy if your performance is stellar. Your core fear is you will be rejected if your performance is not above a certain standard you set. Feeling worthy as a person is constantly out of reach and no amount of performance closes the gap. You either keep coming up short or feel the emptiness of achievement for achievement's sake. You feel like you could show up one day and someone will tell you that you are not wanted anymore, that you are not doing a good enough job. Maybe that idea has not been spoken to you explicitly and it may not even be a tangible thought held in your head, but burning below the surface is a belief that your worth is tied to your performance.

Fear 6: "I am bad."

On the inside, at your core, you believe you are simply a bad person. Maybe you were verbally or physically abused as a child and the only way your mind could make peace with what happened, the only way it could resolve the tension, is to believe you must be a bad person to deserve that. Even if it was never spoken, that lie was wedged in your heart. This shows up in your theology as well. You believe that at the core of who you are you are a sinner and you are defective. Sure, we are all tempted to sin, but that is the surface level of who we are. If your dominating fear is that you are bad, you believe that at the core of who you are you are corrupt, and this is a lie.

Fear 7: "If I mess up, the worst will happen."

You imagine worst case scenarios. There is a constant sense of worry and anxiety going on inside you. It is like the earth could give out from underneath you at any moment. You lean on the value of integrity, but not in a sacred way. It is your fig leaf. You believe that if you do what you are supposed to do then God will do what He is supposed to do and you won't get hurt. Falsely, you believe you will always be in external circumstances that are safe as long as you don't mess up. You want a spirituality that works like a math equation, A + B = C. Cheap spiritual equations might sell books and fill pews, but it develops an attachment to beliefs over an attachment to God. The mystery of God is crowded out.

Fear 8: "If I'm vulnerable, I will be hurt."

You believe if you let your guard down and let people get close to you, they will try to control you. They will try to harm you. So when people get too close you create conflict to push them away. You have learned through pain that if you throw your weight around and aggressively make your presence known, people won't get close enough to hurt you. Shame has energized you to construct a life full of complex maneuvering and wall-building so that others have no idea who you really are. Truth be told, you have been cut so deeply and protected yourself so ferociously, you don't even know who you are.

Fear 9: "I'm nothing special."

You feel like you don't have a unique place in the world. You feel like the world keeps passing you by. Even if someone is talking to you and looking you in the eye, you cannot help but wonder if you are seen or being heard. You suffocate under that kind of despair and you desperately want to know you are unique in the world, so you indulge to comfort the pain. You indulge in an extreme way to prove you are special even if that means going into credit card debt or compromising a committed relationship. You are longing to feel like you have a unique place in this world.

If you make a list of the top 10 hurts you have experienced in life, you will discover those hurts as an attack or threat to your identity. If you analyze your favorite songs, books or movies, they will often reveal which of these nine core fears is your greatest struggle. There is no normal in the process of discernment regarding these nine fears. You may associate very quickly with the core fear regarding your identity, or as you reflect on the theme of your life, you may find you strongly identify with any number of these fears. Yet over time the center of the pain will be revealed.

By enduring the shame of the cross, Jesus faced all nine fears. He became the accursed. He went through the shame so we don't have to be shamed anymore. He felt these so we could get a new name. When there was a blessing from God in the biblical story it was verbal and it was a blessing of identity. It was a new name. Much of the self-sabotaging choices in our life could be summed up as this: You are looking for someone or something to give you a name that answers your fear.

7

DESIRE: WHAT YOU REALLY WANT

One day in the midst of the financially scarce years I told you about earlier, my wife said to me, "Chris, we need to paint this wall." It was as simple as that. She was not looking for a timetable. She was not looking for it to be done that night. All she wanted to know was that I heard her, that it was important to me and that it would be taken care of because it was important to her. Because fear dominated my heart, I heard her demeaning my performance as a husband

and saying I was not worthy. "We need to paint this wall," was interpreted as, "This should have already been taken care of, I do not approve of your performance and I don't think I want to be married to you anymore." She was not demeaning me, but in my insecurity that is what I heard.

My heart's immediate response was to defend itself. When you are hurt in your identity you are inclined to resign or prove what you do not believe. I started listing all of the things I had done to help rebuild our family income, trying to prove that I was performing well. I wanted to regain some sense of worth even though she wasn't attacking me. Now, typically you connect relationally, especially in marriage, with your opposite in personality but your equal in emotional health. So when you are insecure in your core fear you will often unintentionally trigger the other person's core fear. My wife's core fear revolves around her safety. When I defensively raised my voice, it made her feel unsafe. By then we had incited World War III and missiles were crossing in the sky.

The fight had nothing to do with painting the wall. It had everything to do with her knowing she was safe and me knowing I was worthy. When you learn to see conflict this way it changes the way you relate, allowing you to grow through it. When you learn what you really need and desire, you can ask for it from those you love without attempting to manipulate them for a response. I can directly ask for celebration. I can ask for what I have done to be noticed. I can get a celebration of worth from my wife and it can feel amazing. I can enjoy that while understanding it will not be enough to satisfy me.

Shame has wedged a lie in our heart through fear and it has shaped not only how we engage conflict but how we approach life. For most people their life strategy to address their fear and shame falls apart in their 40s or 50s. They run off with someone else or buy some crazy new toy or try some wild new adventure, all as a result of the shame that is manifesting itself in their heart. They are fearfully building a fig leaf trying to get what they need through destructive means. The desire is not wrong. God put in them a desire for whatever their acting out seeks to falsely attain. How the desire is met is crucial and it will never be fully met through human relationships or what can be achieved. So, why not get what you need from Jesus now?

The nine core fears are connected to the fruits of the Spirit as outlined in Galatians 5. The fruit of the Spirit is what we receive through salvation as Jesus inhabits us. Our fears drive us to meet a true desire in a false way. Our fears shape a false understanding of God. The fruits are who God really is and who we can become. We falsely believe we cannot get what we need. When we get what we need from

Jesus, our desire is met and we overflow that very fruit to others. Here is how it works:

Fear 1: "If I'm not needed then I'm not loved."
Desire: Love

If your core fear is you are not loved unless you are needed, your core desire is to be loved just as you are. If you manipulate your work or your relationships so that you are always needed, the life you build will eventually come crashing down around you. Instead, as you get to the root of shame and the lie of your identity you can received the truth of the Gospel that you are loved just as you are. This begins your healing and produces the fruit of the Spirit of love. Receiving God's love will allow you to overflow affection to others as well. You will not need others to need you in order to feel whole.

Fear 2: "If I don't take care of myself, no one else will."
Desire: Joy

If your core fear revolves around being taken care of, the desire you chase is joy. You long to be celebrated. No one ever scolds a newborn for not producing around the house or contributing to the diaper funds in exchange for being taken care of. No, we let the child just be. We celebrate life, we love them and we take care of them unconditionally. If you have never received that kind of caretaking or you had experiences in life that communicated taking care of you was a problem, then that shapes how you approach life. You need to learn how to let your heavenly Father, the perfect caretaker, take care of you. Then you will receive the fruit of the Spirit of joy.

Fear 3: "I don't belong anywhere."
Desire: Peace

If you feel like you don't belong anywhere, you desire peace. You are looking for that place where you are relieved from the pressure and you can breathe. You want a place that makes you feel everything will be OK. When you realize your home and your identity is in God, then you get exactly what you are looking for. Receiving the fruit of the Spirit of peace does not get rid of all your problems because we will always have problems, but it will equip you to solve them. It will give you a resolve to face them head on rather than escape and ignore reality.

Fear 4: "I don't have what it takes."
Desire: Patience

If you believe you don't have what it takes, you need the fruit of the Spirit of patience. You need to hear God say that you have all the time needed to learn new skills. You have what it takes in God and He will teach you how to apply what you do well to other areas of your life. When you hear that truth from God and you receive the fruit of the Spirit of patience, you develop perseverance and become a resilient person. The fruit of patience answers the shame that you feel in your identity and it becomes a root in you so that you become a patient person. If you are an impatient person, it is likely that you believe God is impatient with you. The more you understand that God is patient with you then you will overflow patience.

Fear 5: "I can't perform well enough to feel worthy." Desire: Kindness

If your core fear is that you cannot perform well enough to feel worthy, you need the fruit of the Spirit of kindness. God is not a driving task master pushing you to perform like you push yourself. He is kind. When that fruit takes root in your heart, you will overflow kindness to others. You won't make others feel unworthy if they don't perform, but instead, you will remind them they are worthy regardless of their performance.

Fear 6: "I am bad."
Desire: Goodness

If you believe you are bad, you need the fruit of the Spirit of goodness. There is a basic holiness in people made in God's image and in creation which has been called good by its creator. Your belief that you are bad, broken and corrupt colors how you see everything else. When the fruit of the Spirit of goodness takes root in your heart, you begin to believe at the core of who you are that you are restored in Jesus. You are made new. You hunger and thirst for wholeness at the deepest levels of who you are.

Fear 7: "If I mess up, the worst will happen."
Desire: Faithfulness

If your mind is always running to worst case scenarios, you need the fruit of the Spirit of faithfulness. In the Gospel of John, Jesus said that you can never be snatched out of His hand and who the Father has given Him, He will not lose. You need to hear from the Father the affirmation that no matter what happens to you externally, internally He will always hold you. The fruit of faithfulness and the truth that God will never abandon you becomes the foundation of who you are. Then you will have an internal strength to move into the world and develop loyal commitments and perseverance.

Fear 8: "If I'm vulnerable, I will be hurt."
Desire: Gentleness

If you fear that vulnerability with others will leave you hurt and wounded, at your core you desire gentleness. You want to know that God comes near you but does not force His way into your life. Evil invades but the Spirit invites. God is a gentle God and He invites you into a life where you are no longer victimized by a false perception of Him. That is the root that heals the lie in your identity and produces the fruit that allows you to relax. The same person who once stirred up trouble to keep others at a distance now becomes a gentle peacemaker.

Fear 9: "I'm nothing special."
Desire: Self-control

If you fear that you are nothing special, you desire to be known as unique. In Jesus you are seen for who you are, you are heard for who you are and therefore you can live with self-control. You don't have to pursue life in such a way that you indulge to comfort the pain. With the fruit of the Spirit of self-control, you know you are loved for who you are and you can direct your energies rather than shame directing it for you. You can focus your life.

We focus on the fear first because it is easier to recognize where God wants to build us by reaching clarity concerning what we are really afraid of in that moment. Our ability to build up defenses and numb out the pain is such an advanced skill, we have to face the fear to wake up. This is why transformational stories in the Bible hinge or pivot on whether the individual can face their brokenness. Paradoxically, truth is found by grasping the lies and we live lies more than we tell them. This struggle with fear and desire is shaping your life every day.

If this concept of fears and desires is not understood, it will pollute how you pursue mission and relationships. The kid who is bullied by his dad and bullied in school and who later becomes a police officer so that no one will ever bully him again is pursuing false mission. However, when he experiences God as a gentle God and understands he is safe with God, he becomes a police officer to protect others. The fire fighter who believes he has to rescue people to feel worthy is pursuing false mission. When he goes into it knowing he is already worthy regardless of his performance, he rescues people out of an overflow of who he is.

Once you understand how God heals your identity and makes you whole, the motives for your mission undergo a drastic transformation. It may change your mission completely or it may stay the same, but it will certainly change your motives. And it changes the way you engage your relationships. You may even end some relationships because you no longer need to be needed.

Many people are giving up their true identity, enslaving themselves to their work or someone relationally because they believed a lie. They falsely believed they could only get what they needed from that person or that mission. You can only get what you need from Jesus.

FEAR	DESIRE
If I'm not needed then I'm not loved.	Love
If I don't take care of myself, no one else will.	Joy
I don't belong anywhere.	Peace
I don't have what it takes.	Patience
I can't perform well enough to feel worthy.	Kindness
I am bad.	Goodness
If I mess up, the worst will happen.	Faithfulness
If I'm vulnerable, I will be hurt.	Gentleness
I'm nothing special.	Self-control

8

A WHOLE IDENTITY

An excerpt from my journal in 2006, when I realized I didn't like who I was becoming:

> *I don't live the life I describe to others. I'm frustrated. I'm pulled in too many directions. I can't please everyone. When will I say enough? When can I just be me? What is me? What is the better question? When will I feel my soul is not being picked over?*

I was wrestling. I was trying to figure out who I really was and who God is. What began in 2006 did not come together for a couple of years until I understood the struggle for identity. The process of applying the identity filter is based on learning how to see God for who He is in truth so that you can see yourself in truth. When you understand who you are, it changes how you relate to the world. The lie of shame says you will never be worthy enough, safe enough, or adequately taken care of; that you will never be enough, period. The truth of the Gospel is you are loved for who you are.

If God is not a gentle loving Father, a close brother in the Son Jesus, and an intimate, loving Spirit, then He has been remade in the image of your shame.

God's will for our lives is that we are submitted to the Father, empowered by the Spirit and conformed to the image of the Son. The process He is completing to conform us to the image of the Son is to help us experience a secure identity, find clarity in our mission, and build and attract healthy community. In order to transform our lives, He deals with the shame, the fear and the lies. We ask how we can achieve greater intimacy with Jesus, but this is the opposite of how it works. In John 7 Jesus says that His Spirit is a stream flowing within us. The question is not how to achieve flow or intimacy. The question is what is blocking it? Lies from the hurts block our flow.

How does God unblock our flow? Consider these two scenarios. In scenario one my wife hangs a timeline of my life on the wall to teach my kids about me. It shows where I went to college, who my friends were and even my favorite foods. She also creates a book of facts about me and quizzes my kids. Whoever answers the quickest is rewarded. By completing these challenges they learn more knowledge about me and my life than anyone else in the world.

In scenario two I enter the house and give each of my kids a huge hug. We sit around the dinner table and I ask each of them how they are doing. After dinner we clean up the kitchen together, wrestle in the living room and I tuck them each into bed. I place my hand on their heart and ask them questions about the day, about any hurts or fears or excitement they experienced.

Only one of these scenarios is a true relationship. Unfortunately, most of our Christianity is built around the first scenario. Gaining more knowledge does not ensure your relationship with God will develop. We were created for more than a knowledge buzz about God. You can position yourself to continually experience moments of intimacy.

SECTION 3

lean in

9

LEAN IN

River canoeing in lower-level class rapids could leave you tumbling down the river if you are not prepared. The pressure from the water can bend a canoe around a rock. I saw this with my own eyes on a two-day trip down the Big Piney River. The first day was horrible. I felt like a pinball, bouncing off one rock after another. Every time we came upon a rock we would lean back in fear, trying to avoid it, but then our boat would tip over. It went on like this all the way down the river. We did not paddle down the river. We rolled down it.

At the end of the first day the outfitter examined the beating our canoes had taken on the rapids. We obviously were not the only ones to experience this kind of ride because most of his boats looked like ours. He sat down in the canoe and showed us a trick to help us through day two. Knowing our instinct was to lean away from approaching rocks, he showed us that every time we leaned away, water would rush into the canoe causing us to tip. He suggested we try something counterintuitive. Instead of leaning away from the rock as it approached, he told us to lean into it.

The next day we took another trip down the river with its constant rapids and rocks. We did not flip one time, all because we changed our approach. Instead of avoiding the rocks we leaned in.

When we are aware of the pain, we have to train ourselves to lean into that pain. By leaning into the pain, we resist the temptation to avoid building fig leaves that protect us from the fear we feel regarding who we are. Our feelings are critical to our spiritual development.

Culture tells us we should be dominated by our feelings and whatever you feel like doing, you should just do it. If you feel like hooking up with someone, hook up. If you feel like going off on someone in a fit of anger, go off. Whatever it is you feel like you need to do, don't hold back.

The church culture responds to that broken approach by swaying to the other extreme, encouraging a denial of feelings. We are told that feelings are not important. We are taught feelings make terrible leaders and great followers. This harmful approach encourages us to suppress emotions further. We have created a culture that belittles any expression or possession of strong feelings.

Your feelings are a gift from God. They are a clue and signal to where He is working. If you learn to pay attention to your feelings, you learn to pay attention to the things that you need. It may be something that you need to ask from someone else, or it may be something that you need to ask from God.

One night, after a long day of work, I was eating a bowl of cereal since I had missed dinner with my family. My daughter joined me and slid a note across the dinner table. "Daddy, will you dance with me?" I was going through a phase in my life where I was learning to lean into the rocks, the pain and fear I felt. By learning to lean into the pain, I was also learning to lean into the joy. In that moment, I picked up my daughter, stood her on the chair, held her close and we danced. It was one of the most powerful feelings I have ever experienced in my life. The joy that filled my heart in that moment was so deep because I had processed the pain in my life. The more attuned I was to the pain, the deeper I was able to experience the joy.

Instead of leaning in, most of us have learned to consistently numb ourselves to protect us from the pain. The fig leaves we build because of the fears of who we are keep us from experiencing the joy. Leaning into our feelings opens up the process of exploring and discovering the fears and lies we want to run from. The more we run, the more we condition ourselves to numb out.

I try to teach my kids it is not wrong to feel strong emotion. It is wrong to always act on strong emotion, but not wrong to always feel strongly. Just because we sometimes have strong emotions that we should not act on does not mean we suppress all of the other ones too. During dinner time we will talk about the things that made us feel sad, mad or glad that day. Reflecting on an upcoming event, one of my daughters said she felt excited and scared. This is a point of maturity most adults never reach. You can feel two polar emotions simultaneously and you do not have to act on either of them. You can feel two opposite emotions and both will pass. The more intensely you know the pain, the more you open up your emotional reserves, allowing you to also feel deeper joy.

Our feelings are also how we are made in God's image. God feels. We see that in scripture and we specifically see that in the Gospels with the story of Jesus.

Jesus is our perfect example of what it means to be human. We are made in God's image and through the example Jesus gave us we see that He felt strong emotions. From cleansing a temple, healing in compassion, sitting from tiredness or calling out to the Father in pain, Jesus felt. Like Jesus, our emotions are clues and signals for our journey with the Father. Emotional awareness makes us alert to the work of God in our lives. Our emotions are not God. But they make us aware of a potential connection to Him.

Emotions are gifts from God. We do not deny our feelings, nor are we dominated by them. We are aware and learning. It is powerful to ask yourself, "How am I feeling right now?" You do not have to act on that feeling, nor do you ignore it. You pay attention.

We are told that if we feel bad we must be thinking bad thoughts and if we just think more positively then we will feel better. This is a lie. Sometimes there are things in life that just make you feel sad. Sometimes there are things you just struggle with. It does not mean that you are always thinking incorrectly.

It is not true that we cannot trust our emotions. The truth is our emotions give us insight into where we are right now. They act as a GPS for us. When someone says we cannot trust our emotions it is because they are afraid of their emotions. They are afraid that if they listen to them they will feel pain. Don't worry about distinguishing between emotions and feelings. Instead, be aware of what you feel and why you might feel it.

Your soul is like a house with an infinite number of rooms. You have an awareness of some rooms now, but new emotional experiences lead down new hallways, open new rooms and re-open closed rooms. You are made in God's image. Your soul has an infinite capacity as the temple of God. Deep emotions, whether pain or joy, are opportunities to unlock more rooms. Pain and joy become adventures of exploration with Jesus into who we are.

It is powerful and mature to be able to be aware of your feelings and learn from them without feeling pressured to act on them. My marriage took a significant shift when I learned to notice moments with my wife when I felt vulnerable because I felt like she was unhappy with my performance. In those moments I realize I can either fight with her about it or acknowledge that she is not unhappy with me. Those feelings are only happening on the inside of me. By paying attention I put myself in a space to be aware and learning.

The more you learn to lean into the rock, to lean into the pain and fear, the more you come alive to how beautiful the small moments of life are. You are learning to lean into the things that seem miniscule. Whether it is playing a game with your friends or family, on a walk in the woods, or tucking your kids into bed at night, you are able to be in that moment and celebrate and enjoy.

10

CHILDREN ARE GREAT RECORDERS

One night I was putting my kids to bed and felt there was something as a father I needed to pay attention to. I sensed I needed to apologize because I had not been as emotionally engaged as I wanted to be. I had too many projects going simultaneously and had my head down solely focused on completing them. That night I leaned into those feelings and told my nine-year-old daughter that I was sorry and that the end of the major project was in sight. I reassured her that none of my aloofness was her fault. My neglect had nothing to do with anything she had done but everything to do with how I had organized my life.

This was important for her to hear because most of the fear and pain we feel in regards to our identity has its origin in our childhood. Some of it can be traced back to our young adult years and even some maybe to last week, but the most powerful roots to the lies we believe date back to our earliest moments.

Your earliest experiences have the most profound effect on who you are. You cannot cognitively gain enough knowledge to fix the brokenness of that shame and those lies. It has nothing to do with intelligence. Instead, during those experiences your little heart was trying to survive based on what you saw, felt and heard regarding shame and lies. As a result, you either started overreacting to the world to protect yourself or you repeated the actions that were happening to you. This repetition carries on as we age. You have seen it in stories of abuse, alcoholism and pedophilia. We repeat the shame we have received.

Children are great recorders but terrible interpreters. If my wife and I are arguing over grocery money, a child's natural instinct is to retreat from that space and think, "I

Chris McAlister

wish I could stop growing. Because I can't stop growing, my parents have to spend too much money on groceries. My needs are a problem." Children lack the ability to think through that situation in a way that does not spin it back into their own hearts as a shame-based lie. That lie becomes burned into their hearts and then later in life they lock up, unable to ask for what they need at work or from their community because they believe their needs are a problem.

Somewhere along the way each of us has received lies about who we are. The enemy spun those lies into shame and we were left building fig leaves, trying to get something from life that only Jesus can give us. Additionally, there is something mysterious I have observed in my own children. They have a proclivity to a core fear without any explainable connection to trauma or pain. Since none of us received perfect caretaking, reflection will grow our understanding of how the past has shaped us.

Where your identity is broken, the place you are hurting, is a product of the active and passive wounds accumulated throughout your life. Active wounds happen when someone intentionally comes against you in an abusive or hurtful way, perhaps using their power or authority to make you feel, see or hear something false about who you are.

You interpret the hurt as a lie that shames you. Passive wounds happen when you do not get what you need; when you feel ignored or not cared for. Passive wounds occur when you are not celebrated, affirmed and loved.

I can remember crying in the second grade because my parents were gone so much. So I created a Saturday ritual to remind me the day belonged to my family, not my work. It is to protect me from repeating what I received. Overreacting to those passive wounds I felt as a kid would be to never schedule anything on a Saturday. Instead, I try to balance the week appropriately when other things come up. Learn who you are, what you have been through and how to walk through that.

Learning who you are requires you to acknowledge what you have been through, and to do that you look back at your past. When you learn to lean into the rocks of your life and pay attention to the pain, it will equip you to cast an eye backward to your past and analyze things. Cliché Christianity tends to respond to this with Paul's command in Philippians to forget what is behind and press on toward what is ahead, but Paul was referring to forgetting past achievements. He was not saying you should not reflect on why you are the way you are. You will find Christians who try to hype you up to forget your past and press on, but if you completely disregard your past and what you have been through you will likely repeat the same things that resulted in the mess you are in today.

This is exemplified in Jesus' exchange with the woman at the well. Suffocating in the shame of broken relationships and consistently rejected by men, the woman strategically went to the village well at a time when she could avoid interacting with others. Despite her best planning, Jesus was there. He did not directly confront her though. Evil invades but the Spirit invites. Instead, Jesus asked for a drink, inviting her into a moment where she could face the pain she wanted to run from. Like most do, she attempted to move the conversation away from pain and into a theological debate. Jesus responded, letting her know that God is Spirit and the pain she wanted to run from is the place God was waiting to meet her. Profoundly changed by this experience, the woman left her water jar and ran to the town to interact with others and share about her exchange with Jesus. She ran to the place she wanted to run from. The pain you avoid is the place Jesus is waiting to meet you.

Jesus struggled and hurt like you. There is no part of your daily rhythm and existence where Jesus cannot identify with you. There is no fear, vulnerability, inadequacy, insecurity, or anxiety that He cannot know with you.

Learning to process the grief of your past will add a layer of emotional depth to your life. Through every major section of scripture there is a common theme that challenges us to process our hurts and grief with God and invite Him into the loss. Until we truthfully deconstruct what we have been through, we will not know who we are. Without this deconstruction, who you think you are now is actually the false self that you have created based on lies. You develop a wall, a mask, a persona, a shell to protect yourself from the pain. You ignore reality to prop up your false self. Ignoring reality or numbing the pain deteriorates who you are.

11

ADDICTIONS AND GRIEF

If you were to ask me now what my childhood was like, I would describe to you a completely different picture than if you had asked me when I was in my 20s. It is not that my childhood was so horrible, but I had painted over it with a plastic veneer that was false because of some experiences that introduced shame-based lies. When my brother and I used to talk about our childhood, he would wonder if I was raised in a different family. He remembered conflict and head-butting with dad. I remembered peace. He resented the life of a pastor's kid. I buried the resentment of all the times I did not want to go to church. He wanted more family time. I constructed a false reality of family nights that hardly ever happened as we got older. What changed about those memories is that I learned to lean into the pain and process my past differently.

There are moments from your childhood when you were shamed and exiled from your true identity. In response you created a fig leaf to cover up that pain and you became addicted to the comfort it provided. That fig leaf may be a secret addiction that you indulge in behind closed doors or it could be a public addiction. It may even be an addiction that is praised and encouraged because it is morally inspiring, like how hard you work, how much you serve or that you always say yes when asked for help. Regardless of how it is perceived by others it is still destructive. Addictions are the way we try to quiet the pain in our hearts. It is how we suppress the hurt because the grief brings too much terror to even process.

This is not the example of human development or transformation we see modeled in scripture. In the Psalms intense emotion is expressed towards God and towards people. In these instances the psalmist is lamenting and processing how he feels. We are to engage in this process as well. It is not a public thing. It is between you and God, grieving out the pain, grieving a loss.

The easiest way to recognize the pain is to stop your addictions. Your addictions are there to keep the pain at bay, and when you stop those, the pain comes rushing to the surface. In that pain you will find that a part of you was exiled in childhood and you will never experience wholeness until that part is embraced and welcomed back to your life.

For example, there are some people who believe stoicism is maturity. Most likely, at some point in their life the playful part of who they are was shamed and exiled from their identity. A fig leaf was constructed to cover that pain and it turned into an addiction. Perhaps they are praised publicly for their behavior and accepted by adults because they no longer do childish things. That feedback perpetuates the addiction and it encourages the fig leaf. It keeps the pain at bay, but the identity broken.

When you learn to lean into the pain and become aware of what you falsely believe about who you are you can invite Jesus into the pain so He can repair and restore. Jesus does not give you a false or new memory from your childhood. He walks you back through the pain you experienced and shows you how He was with you in it. Then the part that was exiled is embraced and brought back to the reality of who you are. That is how you become whole again.

I remember a friend reaching out to me in a moment of despair. He stumbled into pornography at a very young age and fell deeper into his addiction as he got older. He grew up as a leader in his youth group and was studying to become a youth pastor but constantly wrestled with the tension between leading others through ministry and the shame of his repeated sin. He was forced to face the tension when his wife found pornography on his computer. He sent me an email saying, "I'm addicted to pornography. I don't know what to do. Can we talk?" I responded simply, "You are not a garbage bag of lust. You are a pool of intimacy." Acknowledging his hurts and pains, over time he learned to go to Jesus and ask for what he needed.

The feelings my friend was experiencing in his addiction were not sinful. There are no sinful feelings. They might be positive or negative, but they are not sinful. The negative feelings are clues to our grief and what we need to process with the Father. Jesus modeled this grieving process in the Garden of Gethsemane in Matthew 26 when He went alone to pray. He processed His grief with the Father rather than applying a tight-lipped obedience that stuffed what He was afraid to lose.

It is through this grieving process you move to wholeness because you unlearn the fig leaves and addictions that you have created to protect you from leaning into the pain. Grieving is critical to unlearning what is not working in your life. If you do not unlearn the shame-based lies, you are setting yourself up for crisis later.

Most people will suffer some kind of identity trauma during their pre-teen adolescence that is often built on something that happened in their childhood. But they suffer through it and learn how to build fig leaves to survive. In pre-teen and teen years, unwise choices are made exploring identity from sexting, cutting and eating disorders. The real crisis is an identity crisis. Then throughout their 20s and 30s they have flickers of questions that pop up. "Should I be doing this job? Did I make the right decision when I was 22? Should I have married this person?" Leaning into those questions and inviting Jesus into the pain is too much to bear so they stuff them.

As they move through their 40s and 50s they learn patterns of numbing out that become a part of who they are. Children's sports become obsessions. Tearing others down distract from facing their own felt shortcomings. Grasping for career significance or the need to constantly be around others keeps them from the stillness that allows fears to surface.

When they hit about 60 years old they finally make a choice. Either they act out in an immature way or become bitter towards life and just decide to suffer it out and complain the whole way.

Is this the path you are on?

My life is dedicated to the mission of helping people through radical transformation. I have seen it happen at every stage of life. I also know most people will not do what it takes to go through it. Whatever stage you are in, the key pivot point is to decide to stop numbing out, finally lean into the pain and grieve what is buried. It does not matter what stage you are in. It is not too late. Make the decision to stop stuffing those questions and stop avoiding the pain.

Make that pivot to lean into the pain and grieve the inferior story the enemy has written for you. Let go of the lies you have been holding onto and choose to live the story that God wants to give you. As you come to know who you are in Him, you will find yourself with beautiful gifts in your mission and community that you would not have had otherwise. But it starts with identity.

Security in your identity is not received through a one-time event. You will have to go back to Jesus over and over and over again to get what you need for your identity. When you know who you are in Jesus, it fuels greater passion and perseverance and clarity in your mission and community. It does not mean mission and community are guaranteed to work out. The only guarantee is in identity. You are God's son or daughter and He is always with you. As you are in touch with the pain and grieve it, God gives you life in your identity. You are gifted with a secure identity to offer your mission and your community. Then you will not go to your mission and community to get what they cannot give you.

So far we have mainly talked about grieving the big things, the larger rocks that show up in your life. As you become more aware of how you feel and build the habit of constantly processing your current moments with Jesus, you will learn to grieve the small stuff too. This is where moment-by-moment transformation happens.

One Saturday – those all-important Saturdays in my life –one of my kids told me there was a flat tire on the van.

They had overreacted to those issues before so I did not think much of it. I finished my breakfast and then checked out the problem. It turned out the tire was completely flat.

It had been years since I last changed a tire and when you don't do something for a long time you tend to take parts of the process for granted. I expected it to be a quick fix and to get on with my Saturday, enjoying it with my family. Needless to say, it did not go as planned.

It took me 30 minutes to gather the necessary tools out and jack up the car. The first time I raised the jack, the car slipped off. Second time, it slipped off again and bent the jack. I had an alternate jack for our other car, but it did not fit right. Irritated, I forced the alternate jack to work well enough so I could finish the project. With the car finally lifted, I took the nuts off but could not get the wheel off. I researched a solution online but the answer I found was a complex, repetitive process that I did not have the patience for. Thankfully, at the bottom of the comments section, one person said he kicked the tire and it fell off. With all of the built-up frustration, it was exactly what I wanted to do.

I kicked the tire, a puff of smoke came out and the wheel fell off. I switched it out for the spare tire and set the car back down. The project had already taken much longer than it should have and was encroaching on lunch so I took a break. When I returned to the garage the spare tire had gone flat too.

This elevated me to a point of aggravation where my judgment and decision-making were less than wise. I hopped into the van and drove with a flat spare tire to the nearest convenience store, completely disregarding any consequences to the rim. I was going to pump up that tire and get to the mechanic no matter what it took.

When I reached the mechanic the process was extended another two hours because they didn't have the right tire. It was 5 p.m. before I was able to drive home and my Saturday was gone.

It is in moments like these where you can grieve the small things and spark momentary transformation. I did not spend the drive home from the mechanic as a despairing Christian, dwelling on how the Saturday was ruined and what lasting scar it might leave on my kids. Nor did I play the insecure Christian, pumping my chest in Jesus' name that everything would be OK. Instead, I invited Jesus into the moment with me and let Him change me. I processed the disappointment of losing much of the Saturday and the anger that this is how I was repaid for serving Him so well throughout the week. As I grieved that out it was affirmed in me that He loved me and I was able to trust Him to bring good out of the situation.

There are some big things you need to grieve in your life. As you grieve the big things, you learn to live in a healthy rhythm where you can grieve the small things as well and this changes the way you process everything. You learn to embrace the seasons of life for what they are.

Think of the stages of a tree. In the springtime it is exciting. There is fruit-bearing and growth. In the summer there is shade and life. Yet the transformation of the spring and enjoyment of the summer are results of the deep work done in the fall and winter.

In the fall, there is shedding and releasing. We were created for a secure attachment to Jesus. When we develop attachments elsewhere, addictions are formed. In the fall season of our lives we let go of old attachments. We shed old leaves in the form of changing jobs or roles. We shed old leaves as we await new motivations for roles that reflect our highest commitments.

The winter is permission to stop. It is a desolate period, a period where we feel isolation. A period where we learn we don't force our way through change. We learn that it is OK to grieve. In the coldness of winter, the trunk of the tree is growing stronger. We learn to read through the Bible appreciating emotions. We embrace the season we are in and the emotional contours of our lives open up. Only as you grieve the past can you imagine a different future.

12

DESIRES RAGE

Desire is the foundation for healthy communication. It is where we learn to speak honestly on an emotional level, where we process our hurts and grief and share the intensity and passion of our joy. This is what it means to meet God deeply, and until you learn to process your grief with God in those private spaces, you are going to remain blocked up spiritually. This space is not for factual communication and is not your chance to influence God. You are speaking in primal language regarding where you are now and what you feel.

In the brokenness of our culture we like to have these primal conversations on reality TV and in front of everyone. We concoct scripted moments where people cuss each other out to increase the drama. The actual words used do not bother me so much, but how they are used and where they are used is important. I have private conversations with God that if anyone heard publicly they would question whether or not I could call myself a Christian. In those conversations I am speaking in primal language, walking through moments with Jesus and telling him how I really felt so He could meet me in the reality of where I am.

Leaning into your pain helps you realize the pain is there for a reason. It is related to passive or active wounds in your life and as you explore those experiences you will notice a theme to those wounds. Aware of the wounds, invite Jesus into them. Stop the addictions and process the grief. As you process the addiction and grief with Jesus your desires are refocused and this is where you experience transformation.

Take lust for example. Lust is a desire focused in the wrong direction. You cannot control every time something might jump out at you but you can be aware of it, invite Jesus into it and focus the desire.

Hate is similar. Some will say that it is sinful to feel any kind of hate, but you cannot control that. You don't have to be dominated by it though and you don't have to deny it. You can be aware and learning. When you invite Jesus into the feeling, you process why you are feeling hatred towards that person, what they did to make you feel that way, what you are afraid of and where you felt threatened in your identity. You refocus the desire and forgiveness overflows. It takes time. You don't have to force it or rush it, but as you grieve what needs to be forgiven, you are able to choose the action of forgiveness.

Depression is a common experience for people. Some find help in counseling. I have personally found therapy beneficial. Depression is a medical reality so medicine does help some stabilize and stair step back into a healthy emotional chemical balance. Some, no matter how hard they try, are left hurting with more questions than answers. I have seen some experience relief from depression by learning to ask the right question. "Why am I depressed?" is the wrong question. The true question is, "What is the source of your anger?" At some level you stuffed something you feel very upset about. You do not have to be in denial anymore. You also do not have to be dominated by anger and unleash it in public forums. You can be aware and learning. Invite Jesus into that moment when you feel your sadness is more intense than normal.

That anger you feel is also connected to desire. There are healthy expressions of anger and we see some in scripture and with Jesus. Those are manifested in a desire to protect. Maybe you are angry about something someone did to you and you are trying to protect yourself. Perhaps you are angry about something someone did to a loved one or a project you are working on and you want to protect those things. However, most of us have been exposed to unhealthy expressions of anger. When I was angry with my wife about her asking me to paint the wall in our house, I was not really angry at her. I was angry because I felt afraid that I was not worthy. I perceived that she was threatening my identity, but she wasn't. It is a powerful practice when you get angry to lean into the rock and ask yourself, what am I really afraid of? Are you really afraid that he won't be home at the time he said he would or are you afraid you will be abandoned? Are you afraid things at work won't turn out like you thought they would or are you afraid that you will be found inadequate, that your needs are a problem, that you are not worthy? Unhealthy anger materializes when we are more self-protective than circumstances warrant.

Without necessarily acting on them, we need to let our desires rage. Desires shape the direction of our life. The more we have access to the core desires (identity), the clearer our direction becomes (mission). Tamed desires position us for a shallow life of sin. When we let our desires rage we become aware of what we really need. When we learn how to get from Jesus those things that we really need, everything else flows from that. We do not have to be afraid of the battle for our identity. We do not have to be afraid of others and how they may threaten us. We do not have to be afraid of what we have been through, the moments we feel like we may have lost or the attacks on our identity.

I wish I was better at constantly living that out. One Christmas I bought new bikes for our kids. I asked my neighbor if I could store them at his house until Christmas Eve because he had extra space and I wanted to hide them. So on Christmas Eve night I went to his place to pick up the bikes. The gas pumps that held the back hatch open on our minivan were broken at the time. Financially, we could not prioritize fixing the problem so we found ways around it. To use the back hatch I had to lift up on the hatch and hold it against my shoulder while loading and unloading. It was heavy and the whole procedure was dangerous. As I was loading the bikes and propping open the hatch, my neighbor started explaining to me how dangerous it was and suggested that I get the van fixed. I told him I had an appointment to get it fixed the next week. I lied. There was no appointment scheduled and no plans to get it fixed.

I did not lie to him because I do not love Jesus. I lied to him because in that moment I heard him threaten my identity. All he was saying is that I needed to fix my van, but I heard him say that I was unworthy. I heard him say I was a terrible husband and father and I could not take care of my family.

This process of leaning into the pain is important because it is where the transformation occurs. That night I was able to process it with God and ask Him why I lied. When you get to the motives, when you get to the fear at the core of who you are, you recognize where the enemy is spinning a lie regarding your identity, and this is where your life changes.

SECTION 4

receive

13

EXPERIENCE SHAPES YOUR BRAIN

One of the most satisfying moments I have experienced as a parent was teaching my daughter how to ride her bike. I wish you could have been there to see it. It was thrilling. She was sitting on the couch and I stood in front of her, explaining the four necessary steps to successfully ride. She meticulously filled in the blanks of her notes and reached such proficiency that she recited each step from memory. I was so proud. I taught my daughter how to ride a bike. She excitedly told her sisters and they begged her to show them how they too could ride a bike. So she sat them down, recounted the four steps and had them copy her notes.

This is ridiculous. I did not teach her how to ride a bike and she did not teach her sisters how to ride. Heads were filled with knowledge concerning the steps to ride a bike, but no bike riding was happening. My daughter learned the steps, but she is not a bike rider. She doesn't have any experience.

It is an easy trap to substitute learning to ride a bike for actually riding the bike as it pertains to our knowledge of God. We need to experience God rather than fill in the blanks about God. Our brains know the difference.

The brain is continually forming in response to our experiences and being shaped by what comes in through our senses. Ultimately, experience shapes our brain. The technical terminology is neuroplasticity. Our brain is constantly forming new neural pathways and as neurons fire together, they wire together. Based on this information, we know that the brain is dynamic. It is not a static organ as we understood it in the past, but a dynamic one that is constantly re-mapping through new experiences[4]. The sensations that we experience as we smell, taste, see, hear and feel build triggers in our life. As often as necessary we should consciously lean into the pain, but because of how the brain works we may not intentionally choose awareness. There may be a smell that causes us to revisit a moment in our childhood and triggers the very pain we have been running from. Or it could be something we see or a sound or a particular place.

These triggers have been unintentionally built and now negatively affect our lives. To the same degree, they can be intentionally built to positively impact our identity. What has happened to us negatively through our experiences can be tipped in our favor so that we positively impact how our brain is being formed.

Our brains want to connect back to our past. I can walk into a meeting in a musty-smelling church and instead of interpreting that as 35-year-old Chris, I am taken back to three-year-old Chris who is bored, tired, frustrated and does not want to be in church all the time. Perhaps you are on the brink of a tirade. You are no longer a 39-year-old mom trying to parent your teenage daughter, but you are in the moment as a three-year-old girl being yelled at by your mom. You think you are experiencing a current moment but your brain is actually taking you to the past. The more intense your experience was, the more your brain wants to save it, record it and remember it for later.

Experiences are shaping your brain and your brain shapes how you experience life moment by moment. The past has shaped your present response. In order to have healing and transformation you need a more powerful present experience than the one from your past. You cannot gain more knowledge about bike riding to experience bike riding. Get on and ride the bike!

The most common self-help in Christianity says that if you think right you will be right. But self-help that does not encompass all of who we are wears off. Forcing a belief on yourself is not a more powerful experience than the fear or shame you might be experiencing.

Picture it this way. You are piloting a plane and the autopilot is set to south. You reach a point when you decide you want to change your life. You want to have clarity in your mission or you want to have peace in your relationships. An irresistible resolve comes over you to take action. You grab the controls, turn it north and begin changing the direction of your life. As long as you have energy you will be able to maintain that new course, but when you wear down and fatigue you will let go of the controls or in airplane terminology, the "yoke". When you let go of the yoke, the plane kicks into autopilot and turns back south because a new direction was not set. All you did was add a veneer of discipline. You forced a behavioral change. The new direction was not who you actually are. You can obtain as much knowledge and information as you want, but until you have a more powerful experience that changes the autopilot or disengages the broken autopilot then you will not see true transformation.

When you have that more powerful experience and when you reset the autopilot, you will no longer have to force an attitude or behavior you wish to have in a given moment. You will no longer react blindly when you feel threatened in moments of relational conflict. Instead, the new yoke will overflow from who you are and you will serve rather than become irritated to get your needs met. You will understand why you feel invalidated and annoyed by some family members. And you will not have to go off or act out so you can be known.

Your brain rewires through a more powerful experience. The woman who was abused as an eight-year-old walks back through those past moments and sees Jesus holding her and weeping with her while it happened. Jesus is not showing himself as powerless. The Bible emphasizes that evil people do evil things. We live in a world where people have free choice. The suffering she experienced was not from Jesus, but He was with her in it. After walking back through the past experience Jesus takes that new, more powerful experience with her to the present day so her identity is not flowing out of that moment in a broken way. Instead, it is flowing out of her in a whole way on the foundation that she knows Jesus is always with her.

This is what it means to be transformed. Jesus is not going to make something up or give you a false memory. He is going to lead you in truth and show you how He was with you in your painful moments. The more you experience healing in the past, the more it overflows to the present for you to get what you need in the moment.

I remember a time I was preparing to speak to an audience of leaders and an image of Jesus washing my feet flashed into my mind. In that instance it lasted a second as I stepped up to talk about identity, but I received what I knew that message was about. It was Christ telling me that I was not speaking to these people to get worth from them. I was entering that room, cleaned by Jesus, to overflow the life I have in Him to those leaders. I was there to give something to them, not get something they could not give me to feel whole.

Jesus is the Great Shepherd. He knows how your brain has been made and He knows what you need. He will walk you through those experiences as you need because your identity is always being shaped. Experiences shape your brain which shapes you. Experiences in your mission and experiences with your community are all shaping you. Remember, we are always processing the journey of our lives along the lines of shame and our core fears. By this we are learning to build a narrative, a common thread, of who we are through every experience of our lives.

Many say character is revealed in difficult times. There is some truth in that but more so, character is shaped by how we process and respond to what we are going through. We can speak more accurately and biblically about difficult times when we understand that our identity is constantly being shaped because of the experiences that are constantly shaping our brains. Through that lens we frame hard times based on potential. The question becomes, are you processing your life through the identity-mission-community filter? When something in your mission fails, do you believe the lie of shame in your identity? When something in your community does not work out like you expected, do you believe a lie about who you are? Are you honestly engaging God emotionally and taking the appropriate actions from there?

More discipline or more knowledge is not the answer for transformation. Dig to the root and reset the autopilot or yoke. Changing your thinking is a part of this but transformation based on your ability or responsibility to change your thinking is shallow self-help. Your feelings and emotions shape your thinking and you cannot choose how you feel. True transformation happens when you invite Jesus into your experiences and He gives you a new yoke.

It is one thing to read truth. It is a completely different thing to go for a walk in the woods and experientially feel that truth and hear that truth and see that truth in something around you. Your brain needs smells, sounds, music, art, the feeling of the wind blowing across your face. Your brain is constantly being shaped and you need a more powerful experience to remap the neurological pathways. That is how we are transformed. It is one thing to know how to ride the bike. It is another thing to feel the wind and freedom. There are many people who know a lot about Jesus. Sadly, most are missing out and living off a few rare moments of riding the bike.

We can have more moments if we ask. My youngest daughter inspires me with her boldness to ask for these moments. One summer I was working heavy on my dissertation. While I was holed up in my home office, deep in thought and hacking away at my keyboard, she ran into the room, spun my chair around, climbed into my lap with her morning breath and gave me a kiss. She expected to be held. In that moment the most important thing to happen in her life was that I drop everything and just be there with her.

It was a beautiful expectation. It is natural, unless wounding or pain happens, for a child to expect to be loved. My daughter's response was an application of the idea that we do not enter the kingdom of God unless we come as children. We must learn to have a more powerful experience in order to have transformation. God has given us a gift. This gift can be used to receive the experiences our brain needs to continually be remapped and transformed and conformed to the image of Jesus. This gift is…

14

IMAGINATION AND SCRIPTURE

Our imagination. It is a gift from God. It is a powerful tool in problem solving – think of scientists who dream up solutions before testing and proving them. It is a powerful tool in relaxation – doctors say one way to calm yourself is to picture yourself somewhere peaceful. And it is a beautiful gift for meeting God in an experiential way.

Be aware that our imagination is a neutral tool. The enemy can and does use it to tempt us. Before we commit a sin, we imagine it. Before it becomes action, temptation appeals to the lies we believe about who we are.

For many people, transformation begins when they realize they have unconsciously been driven by a false image of God who looks on them with whatever shaming emotion they experienced growing up – disgust, irritation, consternation, furrowed eyebrows or general displeasure. They learn it is their imagination at work in a broken and destructive way. The identity filter will help you become consciously aware of what is happening underneath the surface. You are imagining God as the same scorning voice or disapproving face from your childhood.

Recall that the core function of our brain is narrative or story. It is desperate to make a story and will force the facts, even if they are not real, just to try to make sense of things. What we can learn to do with our imagination is fuel the beautiful story God has for us to live. This is much deeper than memorizing a Bible verse for a task-master vision of a false God. You can say over and over to yourself that God is your refuge, but if that is not something you can experience the knowledge will be of no benefit. Handing my doubting child a note that says, "Daddy loves you," and having her memorize it is much different than picking her up and hugging her and finding ways for her to experience that she is loved. An experience of love is going to help her brain remap and when the neurons fire together, they wire together. Imaginatively we receive the story of Jesus and this allows us to be experientially transformed.

Imagination is the key to our struggle with sin. Christianity is often obsessed with defining and avoiding sinful behavior. The New Testament speaks to this focus some but the dominant idea of the New Testament is that in Jesus we can imagine a more beautiful alternative. The pull of temptation on our lives will always be strongest until life with Jesus is experientially more beautiful. Without this gift of imagination we will always be tempted to live a lesser life, to pull back from living with courage in our mission and to hide from being vulnerable and building healthy community.

Scripture is a tool from God to help our imagination fire on all cylinders. It is the word of God to us and the word of God is constantly speaking to help us understand who we are in our identity, find clarity in our mission and build healthy community.

You will organize your identity around your concept of God, so go to scripture and invite Jesus to imaginatively make the scripture real to you. Receive the image and then analyze it based on what you are reading in His word. Discern your imaginative experiences through the filter of what you are reading in His word.

Theologian Alister McGrath said,

> "When dealing with a biblical image it is essential to pause and allow the passage to generate a mental picture. We have to enter into the world of that image. We need to project ourselves into the image, and become part of it, experiencing its richness and implications. Our faith stimulates our imaginations as well as our minds![5]"

When we learn to receive through our imagination how God builds our identity, our behavior is transformed. People who have replaced their broken and destructive lives with a life in church or serving God may have simply replaced one obsession with another. They have never experienced God work deeply at the root level of their heart. When I was 16 years old I was the only employee in a video store. You can imagine the roots of sin that entangled around my heart in that environment. When I went off to college I thought that struggle was behind me. I

open, we receive the experience as God gives it to us. It may be that you are bothered by something now that you do not even realize. You may carry it for a couple weeks and then, in God's timing, read something in scripture that causes it to surface and you invite Jesus into the pain and fear.

Ultimately, fear of the pain holds us back from the space of openness where we are willing to receive the experiences that change our lives. That is why it is so vital to lean into the pain rather than run and hide from it. We avoid those quiet moments because we are afraid the pain will surface. But that pull to avoid those quiet moments is the critical clue to where the Spirit wants to work. God wants to build your identity where the enemy is attacking it. Where the enemy wants you to run and hide or avoid, God wants to speak to you in a still, small voice.

Pain and loss are a part of your story. Instead of letting that be the driving force and focus of your life, God has provided a path of transformation through your imagination. It takes a season of un-learning in order to reflexively trust the Father's goodness. God has given you an imagination to unlearn the lies.

Get this: You cannot out-imagine God's goodness in regards to your identity. You cannot out-imagine the endless abundance of Jesus. You are a partaker of the divine nature.

Many want to believe in abundance regarding their mission and this distracts from the work God does in our identity. They feel a stirring of the Spirit, they read scripture, or they are motivated by God's love and they have this great conviction about how God is going to use them to change the world. It is focused on what He is going to do in their mission or what He is going to do in their relationships. There are no guarantees in mission and community. You cannot out-imagine how good God will be in regards to your identity.

It is the same in parenting. The coddling parents give their kids everything they need to make their mission and community successful. On the other side of the pendulum, parents act distant and aloof to harden their children to the pains of this world. God, our perfect parent, gives us more than we can imagine in who we are and from there allows us to pursue our mission and community. Sure, He will help us along the way, but it will not be without some struggle so that we learn to grow and persevere and develop.

When you learn to receive the truth of who God is in relationship to you, you will experience the intensity of God's delight in you. A lot of Christians want to explain the cross as the only reason God can even stand to look at you. That could not be further from the truth. Perfection of love gazes upon you. Shame causes you to look down. He shows you His delight in you through His face, through His speech and through how He feels about you. The love of God is beautiful and awe-inspiring. Only in the blood of Jesus through the cross can you move past the shame and stand up in the sheer intensity of that love. Imaginative experiences are a gift for God's love to become our defining reality.

Chris McAlister

15

SEE / FEEL / HEAR

In the Gospels we discover that Jesus is not distant or untouchable. He eats and drinks with those who are around Him. We can have this same kind of closeness to Jesus today. The word of God tells us that Jesus is seated at the right hand of the Father and we are seated there with Him. Our objective reality is that we are seated in the Heavenly realms with Christ. It does not always feel that way but it is the truth. Objectively, we are continually experiencing God and knowing Him. Every time the word "know" is used in the New Testament in reference to our relationship with Jesus, it is referring to knowing Him in an intimate way, to experientially encounter Him. It is riding the bike, not just learning about riding the bike.

Three channels – seeing, feeling and hearing – open up your ability to experience God. One of those will be stronger for you and one will be weaker. For me, feeling is the hardest to experience but seeing is very strong, hence my experience when I saw Jesus wash my feet as I was walking on stage to speak. For you it could be completely opposite. Wholeness begins when you learn to lean into your strength, and growth becomes catalytic when you ask Jesus for help with the places you are weak. I can easily see Jesus delighting in me. In my imaginative moments we are sitting around a camp fire, me in one chair, Him in another, and He is just delighting in me. To a lesser degree I can hear Him, but I struggle with feeling. Sometimes we can find resources that help us activate our weaker senses. I have a certain song that helps me feel. Maybe there is something that helps you see or hear.

Larry Hurtado, one of the key scholars in the early church and a specialist on early Christian community, studied the phenomenon of the massive base of Jews converting to Christianity. He found that one of the key factors in this explosion was revelatory experience[6]. Through the Spirit these people were feeling, seeing and hearing Jesus. The ascension had occurred and God came to live inside them. They became the temple of the Holy Spirit, making Jesus real to them.

Two common ditches keep this emphasis on experience from being more widely taught and openly practiced. The first is an overly willful application of this teaching. It is attempting to force an experience rather than remaining open to receive one. The second ditch is at the opposite extreme, a passive approach to imagining. Movements on this side would gather on Sunday morning and sit quietly. No one would speak until someone felt led by the Lord to speak. These two approaches have impacted every strand of the church from Catholic Mysticism to the Puritans.

The Puritans used a phrase I have found very helpful. "Invite Jesus into..." wherever you are[7]. God is there already but this phrase helps you become aware of His presence. When you feel distressed, threatened, angry or bothered, invite Jesus into that space. Ask Him what He really wants you to see, feel or hear about the emotions you are having in that moment. Ask Him what you are really bothered by or upset with or where you are really being threatened. You will discover that you are not bothered by that unexpected bill, but your agitation is connected to a lie you believe regarding shame in your identity. You will find that it will always be about the root, not the fruit.

I invite Jesus into my current reality as a means of becoming aware of how I can see, feel and hear the Father at work around me. Jesus, when He talked about His relationship with the Father, talked about seeing (John 5:19), feeling (John 15:9-11) and hearing (John 12:49) Him. Jesus is our example and the Spirit empowers us to be conformed to the image of the Son. To the degree that Jesus saw, felt and heard the Father, He provides the example for the kind of experience we can have.

Yet if our experience does not take us to the Jesus revealed in scripture then it is false. If we believe in a God that is different than who Jesus taught God to be then our understanding of God is false. If our understanding of God is false, be careful. Holy things do more harm than good when our understanding of God is misinformed. To protect us, He has given us the gift of imagination enlivened by the Spirit for the healing of our past, the enjoyment of the present and the anticipation of the future when we will no longer need our imagination. At any moment we can go to Jesus and get what we need.

When I first became aware of the power of this tool I would have moments when I would lock myself in the bathroom and process this. I would ask Jesus to use my imagination to make what I knew to be true objectively as I was seated in the Heavenly realms, also true to me subjectively in that specific moment. My kids thought I had a bladder problem, but what I was doing was escaping to a space where God could use my imagination to help me experience truth. I operated this way for about a year, but as you mature in this process you reach a point where you will not have to retreat. You will be able to call on this in the moment.

It is sad to see most Christians living their lives off of one or two experiences when scripture became real to them in their imagination, usually from a conference or a retreat. They hit a spiritual mountaintop and try to hang onto that experience for as long as it will fuel them. It is sad because they do not realize that they can internally engage this mountaintop whenever they need it. As you are hanging on to these one or two experiences, the fresh water that was inside you becomes stale and what you overflow to others is stale. You do not have to live off a stale experience. You can access the well at any time you need it to get from Jesus what you are lacking. You can continually cache new imaginative experiences with Jesus that you can draw on repeatedly. You can continually reorient your identity around His identity.

16

NEW SELF

Growing up, I hated the role of being a pastor's kid. There was really no way around it and I despised it. Because of that strong emotion towards always being the pastor's kid, I chose a negative way of living it out. I was rebellious just to prove I did not fit the role I felt forced into and that I loathed. When I was in the fifth grade our family routine was to be at church at least three nights a week. I hated that so much I stashed my skateboard in the station wagon before we left. When my parents thought I was at children's choir, I snuck out the back and skate boarded in the parking lot. In seventh grade the junior high pastor kicked me out of the room and I ran away and hid up in a tree. In high school I did stupid things just because my peers dared me to. They taunted me with the pastor's kid label and I responded by doing even more outrageous stuff just to prove that was not who I was. It was all an overflow of the insecurity and fear I felt in my identity.

I later realized that when you follow Jesus, it is death to the old self. It is death to the self that is laced with fears and has to prove, and you come alive in the new self, the true identity of who you are in Jesus. When you can let go of the false identity, dying to the old self, your life has changed.

Unfortunately, many teach that we must hate ourselves, we are trash and Jesus is all that matters. We are told to make it all about God because self does not matter. "Everything is for God's glory" is used as a stamp to authenticate destructive teaching which de-values personhood. John 3:30, "He must become greater; I must become less" is used to inflict shame. If you read the context, John's statement was not one of personhood. It was one of mission. He was saying that Jesus' ministry must increase now and his must decrease. John the Baptist was pointing forward to Jesus and now that Jesus was on the scene, it was time for him to decrease his ministry.

A lie is taught that the only way God can look at you is through Jesus, but the Bible does not say that. The Bible affirms the truth, that we are worthy because God created us, that Jesus died for us because He loves us and that we matter.

The opposite extreme is just as broken. On the other end of the spectrum there are Christian circles that want to make it all about you. They say that if God loves you then you will be healthy, wealthy and have everything you need. They teach that mission and community will be everything that you ever dreamed it would be.

Culture also has a view on this and it is presented as, "Be yourself." Society trumpets it on articles of clothing and upholds it as a life mantra. This is a very shallow, vacuous approach. You will feel small moments of relief in trying to "be yourself" but it does not give you a compass, a center and a place from which to orient yourself. Being yourself is not a solid core you can continually draw from.

The truth is found in the tension of the extremes and focuses on identity. In Ephesians 4:21-24, Paul deconstructs the idea that we are trash and Jesus is all that matters:

> "You heard about Christ and were taught in him in accordance with the truth that is in Jesus. You were taught, with regard to your former way of life, to put off your old self, which is being corrupted by its deceitful desires; to be made new in the attitude of your minds; and to put on the new self, created to be like God in true righteousness and holiness."

Christianity is not the destruction of self. It is the purification and amplification of the new or true self. Our old or false self is corrupted by deceitful desires when we go to the wrong places to get what we need in our identity. When our self is in Jesus, it is made new. Paul offers us a perfect way to not put on this super spiritual persona and to not be stuck in this empty nature of culture. We put off or die to the old self, the self that is stuck in condemnation, in fear, in shame and the ways we build our identity around mission and community. We put on the new self that we build around faith, hope and love.

This transformation is not instantaneous though. There is a process and it is a hard process because you are letting go of deep attachments. Many of these attachments were formed to survive painful experiences in your life. You could not control your mom's angry outbursts, but you could numb the pain with binge eating. You never chose to have your sexuality awakened at too young of an age by your older brother, but you could numb the pain with cutting.

Before you can live in the new self, there is this middle space where you have nothing to hold onto. It is the dark night of the soul that Christians have talked about throughout church history. Look at any story of transformation in scripture and you will see this middle space in the process. Joseph was in prison. Jacob was alone on a dark riverbank. Moses was in the wilderness 40 years. Elijah was in a cave. Jonah was in a whale. Jesus experienced it in the wilderness following the baptism. I experienced it on a wooden deck in my backyard. This middle space is a space of grieving and letting go of who you have been and making peace with no longer having any false external security to hold on to.

We have spent our lives constructing fig leaves and building our identity around things related to our mission and community. Let go of this security blanket of the pretend self in order to move to the new self, where you are comfortable in who you are in Jesus. It is such an amazing, freeing feeling to know you are loved for who you are and where you are, and to be in a place where there is nothing you can change about your life to be more loved than you already are. This new self will provide a new focus to your mission and a new way to relate in your community.

I noticed my old self when I took my three-year-old daughter out to lunch for her birthday, just me and her. I was about to ask her a series of questions about how much fun she was having hanging out with me and how glad she was that I took her out to lunch. In my head I recognized the real message of the questions. I should have just asked her what I really wanted to know: "Aren't I a great daddy to take time out of my day to spend with you?" At the root, I was looking for worth from a three-year-old. In my old self I served to get what I needed for my identity, worth. In the new self it flipped to where I can be present with my daughter just to love her. It is no longer about me getting what I need. It is about celebrating and loving her.

The path to maturity will include some dark knights and moments where you learn to let go of old ways. Over time you will learn to live out of the new self, secure in who you are in Jesus and overflowing to a clear mission and healthy

Chris McAlister

community. The false self is your past. The true self is your future. Either of these can be actualized in the present.

SECTION 5

rest

17

LIFE ISN'T WORKING

With young children in the house, breakfast on Saturday mornings tends to become a production. One morning I could not find anything to fix. Sifting through the cabinets, I grabbed some random ingredients and ended up with oatmeal, cinnamon and sugar.

Much in parenting is how you sell it, so I was trying to have fun and market it as the next big thing, hoping my kids would enjoy it. I branded it as Cinnamon Cookie Oatmeal and bragged about it to my wife. When I served it, my youngest daughter took one bite, made a disgusted face, pushed it away from the table and refused to eat any more saying, "I don't like it."

I have noticed throughout my conversations with Christians that many of them have a massive disappointment in their experience with Christ. If they could be honest about what they feel they would say, "I don't like it." That disappointment stems from their identity being built around their mission or their community, rather than truly understanding who they are. The identity filter is a simple filter to process your life, but you cannot take shortcuts. It takes time.

When you build your identity around anything that can be gained or lost, you set yourself up for a crisis. There are no guarantees in mission or community. The only guarantee we have is found in our identity. God loves us and is with us all the time. When we try to meet our needs through mission or community, we construct idols and a cycle of disappointment is set into motion. Things come crashing down, we feel like we don't measure up and then we start over. We try a different tactic or we quit and move on to something else, but the cycle continues.

This cycle begins with comparison. We see what everyone in our relational network and our expanded network is doing and how we measure up. We see their possessions and accomplishments, and with social media we see the edited parts of their life. And we feel our inadequacy. It can be dangerous.

Make a careful exploration of who you are. We can be easily distracted by comparison and comparing ourselves to others erodes who we are. God is the most joyful being in existence and He lives in you. Through an understanding of who you are and the power living inside you, you can be your creative best in your own life without needing to compare yourself to others. Your ambition and drive is healthy when you are focused on being the best possible you. Insecurity means you need to be seen by others as the best.

Our insecurity in who we are means we suffocate under the pressure of the roles we fill. We all operate in multiple roles – spouse, parent, sibling, employee, neighbor, etc. – but none of those roles should define who we are. Sadly, well-meaning Christians can apply pressure for unattainable roles focusing on oppressive performance. From being a Proverbs 31 woman to a teenager maxing out spiritually to impress his parents, the role suffocates rather than inspires.

When you build your identity around those roles you might drive yourself to a perfect standard. If you feel like you cannot reach that standard, shame will lead you to give up and choose a negative, rebellious identity so you don't have to live under the pressure to be perfect.

We see examples of this in people that flip out and suddenly switch gears. It is the dad who walks out on his family with little or no apparent urging or the employee who drops everything and quits his job with no leading from God. They have internalized a perceived external pressure and they are suffocating under the role. They are desperate for relief and it is easier for them to choose the negative response and escape, rather than stay on the exhausting treadmill of pushing themselves to perform.

Through the identity filter, when we know who we are and our identity is whole, we can learn to move in and out of these roles and survive in varying circumstances regardless of our performance or how we feel. You can have a bad day at work but shift gears and bring who you are as a secure parent into the home. You can have a fight with your spouse right before a work meeting and shift gears into a different role.

One key element to being able to move in and out of roles is the ability to understand the appropriate personas we need in each role. We use personas, or wear masks, to be the person we are supposed to be in that moment. Out of insecurity, the persona becomes rigid or the mask becomes fused to who we are and we do not know how to be any other way. When you have a secure identity and know who you are, the personas become a tool to be used as needed. They serve you. You do not serve them. It is not being fake. It is being in the moment and offering what the situation demands.

For me as a pastor, on Sunday mornings I need to be the optimistic, passionate leader, but there are also times I am with my church and I don't need to be any of those things. I can move out of that role and be playful, silly Chris. As a husband there are days when I can be tired, weak and vulnerable with my wife, but there are also times when she needs me to be provider, caretaker and carry a heavier load. When you know who you are, when you are secure in your identity, you can move in and out of roles as needed in a healthy way without them defining who you are.

We are set up for crisis when we do not know who we are. We try to get what we need from each other and that sparks conflict. James says, "What causes fights and quarrels among you? Don't they come from your desires that battle within you?" (James 4:1) Selfishness is attempting to get from others what you need and can only get from God. When you look to someone else to fill those needs you put pressure on them to be God in your life, but they will never be able to fully meet that need related to the core fear of your identity. Only God can do that.

When you are secure internally with who you are in Jesus, people around you can freak out externally however they need, while you remain stable and secure without being pulled into conflict. The external chaos they create does not have to be an internal threat to your identity.

18

THE ENEMY'S PLAN

A couple years after the iPhone came out I was still suffering under the misery of my razor flip phone due to financial constraints. In my desire to make an upgrade I dreamt up a long list of great reasons of how an iPhone would make me more productive, my work more effective and my life generally easier. Near Christmas I found out that my wife shared that information with my parents. That excited me because my parents tend to be especially generous around the holidays. Right before Christmas they showed up with piles of presents and one little gleaming box had my name on it. It was exactly the size and shape of an iPhone. I was so excited. Outwardly I was trying to play it cool but inside I felt like a little kid again. My daughters were opening all of their presents and I anxiously wanted to hurry them along so we could get to mine. In my head I had already downloaded my favorite music and bought a dozen apps that were going to change my life.

When it came time for me to open my gift, I tore off the wrapping paper faster than a child revealing a new bike. But the anticipation was blunted and first-world despair set in as it became clear the item in the iPhone-shaped box was not an iPhone. It was a Christmas ornament. I was so disappointed. I had set my hopes so high for what it might be and came up short.

This same range of emotions can explain the disappointment many feel with Christianity. They get their hopes up only to find frustration. They have tried harder and it's not working. They have tried to gain more knowledge, they have tried to serve more, they have tried to change churches, they have tried all the different tactics and it is just not working.

The church exists to lead people to a true identity in Jesus, which will overflow into true mission, which will attract and build healthy community. The problem is that so many who speak for God seem to have a false sense of identity. They build who they are around possessing the right beliefs so they can belong. They have been sold a lie that they are not worthy unless they are effective. They get distracted by comparison and they suffocate. If you ask Christians why they serve, most will tell you they want their life to count and they want to have an impact. What they are doing is trying to get something from their mission for their identity. Their mission or service cannot give them enough to make them whole.

With a secure identity, your life already counts regardless of mission. When you are living from a false identity, you pursue a false mission and you build a false community. This is the enemy's plan for your life. We saw it with Jesus in the wilderness after the baptism. Satan is going to attack you in your identity and sell you a lie about who you are. He is aiming to hurt your heart, and when he gets you to hurt in your identity you will resort to proving. The quickest way to recognize what someone does not believe about themselves is when they try to prove it to you.

FALSE IDENTITY > FALSE MISSION > FALSE COMMUNITY

Hurts > Inadequacies > Pretenses

Prove > Frustrations > Judgments

Proving manifests itself when you either aggressively power up or passively resign. For the people aggressively powering up, they are trying to prove it actively. For the person resigning, they opt to be the wallflower and refuse to put themselves out there or be vulnerable so the world cannot hurt them. Paradoxically, the world has already hurt them and that is why they are disengaged.

When we start proving, we put ourselves in this spin cycle of frustrations. These frustrations are a result of the inadequacies we feel in our different roles and the pressure of moving in and out of the different personas. One byproduct of these frustrations is that we read into other people what is happening in our heart. This is judging. The hurts you feel make you frustrated in your roles and you eventually tear down the community around you through judgments. Proving severs your ability to connect with your community and disrupts the work in your mission. Rather than moving in and out of roles with a secure identity, you deteriorate.

When you get stuck in this spin cycle of frustration, you will devote more energy to hiding behind the fig leaves. Your false self becomes more time consuming to maintain. Exhaustion overwhelms you since there are always more people to convince. The personas we live become fused to our identity to comfort and mask the pain we feel. This is all part of Satan's plan. He wants you in a space where you are proving, you are frustrated and you are judging so you will live out of a false self. When he has you living out of a false self you will have a false mission and attract a false community. He wants you to build your identity around your mission and your community so you are distracted, blocked up and not living God's plan for your life.

19

GOD'S PLAN

I have had some amazing experiences where Scripture has come alive through the gift of imagination. These experiences help me to learn to live out of a secure identity. There are plenty of moments when I still feel insecure, but these are reminders for me to receive from Jesus what I need. And I do that... much of the time.

In 2010 I was under a tremendous amount of pressure at work. My wife and I got into an argument, and instead of inviting Jesus into my insecurity, I punched a door in our house. In front of my kids.

For the record, I have never laid a hand on my wife in violence. And as an aside, if you are in a space where there is violence in the home then you need to get out and get to a safe place. Take immediate steps toward separation to pursue reconciliation.

That was not the case in this scenario but it was an act of immature, unbridled anger in front of my kids and they were afraid. I felt terrible. Guilt – feeling bad about what you do – and shame – feeling bad about who you are – were mixed up in my heart and I sensed the enemy trying to spin this into a lie about my identity. I felt him trying to convince me that I had to quit the church and that I was no longer worthy to be a pastor because of this. Processing through the identity filter, I was aware that none of that was true.

I sat my kids down and explained to them it is not wrong to feel strong emotion, however there are times when it is immature to act on strong emotion. That is what I did and it was wrong. I apologized. I also told them they never had to feel like they had to hide what I did from anyone just because I was a pastor. Being a pastor's kid is a role that was forced on them and I never want them to feel like there is an expectation they have to live up to because of that.

Because I had learned to separate who I am from what I do, I was able to repair the tear with my kids and turn a broken moment into a deep, instructive moment.

I still struggle and I can tell a hundred other stories where I did not seize this kind of opportunity. I want you to understand that when you are in a space where you are trying to prove externally to the world and to yourself who you are, you are living the enemy's plan. There is a better plan.

Your true home, your true identity, is in Jesus. Whatever you are trying to prove through powering up or passively resigning, God wants to give you the gift of life in Him through receiving. This is God's plan.

He wants you to become aware of the hurt. The same way He asked Adam and Eve to acknowledge where they were and the same way He asked Jacob to say his real name, God wants you to admit who you truly are and where you are hurting. Our constant choice is between the false self or the true self. Our wakeup call occurs when we become aware that we have lived lies more than we have told them.

When you are aware of the pain, you invite Jesus into that and it changes your mission. When Jesus is with you in your pain, you get from Him what you need and overflow healthy mission to others.

After you invite Jesus into the pain, you discerningly share it with your community. When you share the places you have been hurt and where you have needed Jesus to be your comfort, it relaxes the environment relationally. It subsides the judgment because everyone realizes we are all on this journey together.

Through the identity-mission-community paradigm we understand that our identity is always safe and secure regardless of what happens. People say that the safest place to be is in God's will. I hear people counter that statement by saying God's will should not be safe because when you are doing God's will you have to be ready for something dangerous. The truth is that your identity is always safe in Jesus. From there you can pursue mission. That mission may not always work out like you think it will, but even though things are dangerous externally in your mission, internally you can always be safe in your identity.

When you have peace in who you are, you overflow life and have passion in your mission because your mission is not wrapped up in what you need for your identity. You can pursue what you do with determination and perseverance and appropriate intensity. Your mission overflows life where you have received comfort in the pain of your identity. Your pain reveals passion. Your frustration becomes focus. Your suffering shapes how you serve.

IDENTITY > MISSION > COMMUNITY

Aware > Invite > Share

Peace > Passion > Understanding

A focused mission overflowing from a secure identity will attract and build healthy community. Biblically, when God transformed a community, it was built on an individualistic experience. We need community but we need to meet God in the wilderness first. Then, within that healthy community, you can be vulnerable and weak when necessary which builds stronger connections. This does not mean you have to share everything. Over-sharing can be unhealthy if you are only trying to test someone's commitment to make you feel better about yourself. No, you do not have to be brutally honest all the time, but you also do not have to give into the temptation to run and hide or cover up who you really are. Jesus understood this tension perfectly, balancing the times He was amongst the crowds and the intimate moments with the disciples and how much He shared with each. With a secure identity you can be engaged in the moment and give to the community exactly what it needs rather than take from it what you need to feel whole.

When you apply the identity filter to your life, even to the smallest moments, it will open up the places you feel vulnerable and weak and flip them so you can be engaged in mission and discerningly intimate in community. This is God's plan for your life, that you would be conformed to the image of Jesus.

realized later that I just traded a broken sexuality for an obsession with ministry. That became the new addiction. It was not until I had no fulfillment in mission that I journeyed deep to the root level of my identity. The deepest level of change happens when we receive imaginative experiences that heal the fear and shame.

Change is not about striving to be secure in your identity or striving for your shame to be healed or striving to be free of fear. This is about receiving. The Great Shepherd can and will lead you through this exploration. Receive the gift of imagination that He wants you to use to remind you of who you are. Allow Him to direct how He wants to heal your past. That healing comes from an experience.

Keep in mind, this identity message is for you to experience a secure attachment to Jesus, not an attachment to the experience. The experience facilitates the deep attachment to Jesus which answers the lie you believe and fear you have about your identity. You belong, you are loved, you are worthy. You need the experience to soak those truths into your identity, but an openness to receive these gifts protects you from worshipping the experience itself. Some might be nervous about this concept of an experiential encounter with Jesus. Some might react immaturely, worshipping the experience. When we remain

20

OVERFLOW

When you learn that you can approach Jesus in the middle of a moment in your day and experientially get from Him what you need, it changes your prayer life immensely. Prayer becomes a conversation. Prayer becomes a gift to receive. Prayer becomes speaking, waiting and listening. Prayer becomes a protest you voice.

Many people growing up in the church are taught some method of working God over when they pray. For me, I was taught about ACTS: Adoration, Confession, Thanksgiving, Supplication. It was a framework we were to use in prayer to be sure we covered all the bases. Think what it would sound like if my kids talked to me the way we talk to our heavenly Father. Imagine one of my daughters saying, "Daddy, you are the man. I know you told me to brush my teeth before I went to bed last night, but I didn't. I'm sorry. By the way, thank you for buying the toothpaste. I really appreciate that. Will you please fill up my sippy cup?" As a dad listening to this I am wondering why she didn't just ask me to fill up her sippy cup.

When you learn to see yourself for who you are and realize the goodness of Jesus, you don't have to work God over. You no longer have to worry about the lists. There is no right or wrong way to approach Him. When you feel yourself being threatened in your identity, it is an invitation to intimacy. That becomes your prayer. You go to Jesus asking for an experience in that moment that helps you feel safe and secure in who you are.

I vividly remember one Sunday morning before I was about to preach feeling especially anxious and nervous about the service. There was a fear of identity at work in me which was going to cloud up how well I could do in my mission and in building community. I sat in the front row and invited Jesus into that space. I told Him I felt afraid that I would not perform well enough to feel worthy. I asked Him, as the Great Shepherd, to lead me through that fear and to help me receive an experience to comfort the pain. In that moment I saw a big tree with kids running around it and Jesus playing with them, and I received this message from Him: "When you go up there to preach in a few minutes, we will all be playing in here. Go up there and play. I love you."

I still go back to that image many Sundays and draw from that experience. I do not worship the experience. I still practice discernment to be sure the message I receive points to Jesus. But I can and do draw from it regularly. I will continue to draw from it until the Father gives me a new experience. When I get what I need in my identity, I will have clarity in my mission.

Part of being conformed to the image of the son Jesus is to live with the same amount of focus and passion He had in regards to the clarity of His mission and building community. In the book of Luke we see how laser-focused Jesus is on Jerusalem. Everything He does points towards Jerusalem. His mission is not about healing everyone in every town, although He does heal many along the way. It is not about teaching everyone who wants to learn, although He did teach many along the way. It was all about getting to Jerusalem. We see the same kind of focus and clarity as He built and attracted community. The misery of an insecure identity is that you will have an un-attempted mission in your life or you will be distracted by the wrong one, and you will lead a withering or non-existent community.

You will be able to endure the deserts when you process your life through the filter of identity. As much as we can imagine the experience of God's goodness to us regarding our identity, there is a mystery in those times when God feels farther than the moon. It is in these deserts that we learn to allow the true desires of who we are and what we want to surface. You cannot leave the desert on your own strength. It will disorient who you are and you will never be the same afterward. In these deserts you can be rigid, power up and will yourself out of it, you can disengage and just give up, or you can make peace with the fact that you are in a desert and be aware and learning. Hope breaks through when we learn acceptance. Jesus accepts us for who we are and where we are. Out of that we do not live in self-righteousness or self-hate, but in the desert we experience a re-centering of our identity. We are re-learning who we are. We are re-learning who Jesus is.

Jesus heard about who He was twice explicitly in scripture, at the baptism and at the Mount of Transfiguration. Every time the Bible says He went to a solitary place, it is the same word for this idea of the wilderness. If Jesus needed to walk into these solitary places multiple times, how much more do we need the rhythm of contemplation and action in our lives? Then a pattern emerges. As we have experiences with God, it leads to clear action. You can either walk yourself into the desert experiences or you can keep stuffing the big questions that arise and be forced into the desert by the troubles of life. Yet even in the deserts that are a result of our own poor choices, Jesus is with us. Throughout the Gospels Jesus affirms personhood without endorsing behavior. He ate with the tax collectors but never supported their financial manipulation. He is with you.

When you process your life through the filter of identity, you will be able to resist the easy way out in building who you are around behaviors or beliefs. Ultimately, it will challenge you to shift the way you think about Christianity. Building your identity around having the right beliefs or behaviors is not a true experience with God. Christianity is not about your strengths being forced on others around you. It is about learning to be vulnerable and receive in the space where you feel weak.

When you process your life through the filter of identity, you will be able to bring the fullness of who you are in Jesus into every space of your life. When chaos closes in around you, you will be able to resist the temptation to prove through powering up or resigning. You will find in Jesus that the vulnerable parts of who you are will be made secure in your identity with Him.

I had a professor in my doctoral program who grasped everything we have talked about in a very deep way. She was in her 60s and experienced a depth with Jesus that seemed so rare. She was authentic and a little rough around the edges because of her understanding of how to honestly process as life happened. One day she told us a story about watching a mother verbally rip a child apart in a department store. The mother tore her kid down with heavy doses of shame. As the mom walked away and the enemy was spinning a lie into the boy's heart about who he is, my professor walked up behind him and embraced him. The boy fell into her arms. She sat down with him in the middle of the department store and whispered in his ear: "As real as this hug is to you right now, Jesus is always there to give you what you need. Come to him and ask." She lived first gear first and wanted to help the little boy do the same.

That is the SightShift process.

Chris McAlister

NOTES

1. For more exegetical information on Luke 4 see www.chrismcalister.com/book-Luke4

2. For more information on a technical understanding of identity see www.chrismcalister.com/book-identity

3. I am attempting to rework contributions from fields of personality development and typology. Early on I was influenced by the Riso book. After I had already done work making a larger Biblical connection I discovered the book by Richard Rohr that may be helpful to you:

Riso, Don Richard and Russ Hudson. 1999. The wisdom of the enneagram. New York City: Bantam.

Rohr, Richard and Andreas Ebert. 2011. The enneagram: a Christian perspective. New York: CrossRoad Publishing.

4. For more information on an understanding of the brain in regards to the re-mapping of neural networks see www.chrismcalister.com/book-brain

5. McGrath, Alister. "Encountering Biblical Spirtuality". Metamorpha.com. October 1, 2011. http://metamorpha.com/blog/2011/10/01/alister-mcgrath-encountering-biblical-spirituality/

6. Hurtado, Larry W. Lord Jesus Christ: Devotion to Jesus in earliest Christian community. Grand Rapids: Eerdmans. (see page 64-65)

7. I cannot remember where I first came across this phrase but for a brief historical snippet see www.chrismcalister.com/book-history

ACKNOWLEDGMENTS

What started with an idea over 5 years ago would not be in book form with out the support of my wife Brandi. She has consistently been there throughout the craziest ups and downs. I would not have chosen for us to go through those but I feel humbled at her resiliency. When at the bottom she still believed and championed our pursuit of mission. When my ideas weren't communicated with simplicity regarding the content of this book she inspired to keep going. When the finances didn't make sense she cheered the big vision and the small details for what it took to launch SightShift. Thank you for taking this path of risk with me and keeping our home a refuge.

And for my three precious ladies, Ashlynn, Madi, and Brae, everything that jolts my heart in fresh appreciation of God's love seems to so often originate in my relationship with you. One of the most sacred adventures of my life will be cheering you on in your adventure. I'll always celebrate the uniqueness of who you are and your journey.

Bret, there's a reason your name is on the cover. When I started compiling the extra research post-dissertation in February I was unaware at how time consuming the process of distilling down to the key content would be. I also knew I needed a lot of help translating what was in my head as spoken teachings to written teachings. You dove in, helped the voice stay consistent, and gave a herculean effort to get us here. When do we do the next one?

Tim and Adam, you give me courage. Tim, you've been there when most backed off at what seemed to be some kind of curse on my life. You've spoken hope when I was most afraid. You've helped me laugh when I was sad. I'm so thankful for the calming presence you are to help us swing easy. SightShift will never be what it can be without your leadership gifts. Adam, your authenticity shaped so much of the beginning pursuit of SightShift. Your authenticity shapes so much of SightShift now. The gift of who you are makes us whole. The savvy of your skills keeps us relationally focused. Let's play! Both of you were there at that first overnight retreat. You brought people. You served. Thirty-nine years to go!

Allie, the gift of your passion, skills, and energy to help our work communicate with the quality you emulate is celebrated. You've taken us further, faster than we would be able to go on our own!

Discovery Church, thank you. Your passion to learn who you are in Jesus, go after mission, and build community inspires me. Healthy churches are laboratories of experimentation as the Spirit is followed. Your embrace of the way we risk and grow helps me lead from the healthiest part of who I am. You don't pressure me to live up to a role but follow as we seek God together. Thank you Discovery team! I know we walk a fine line between being overwhelmed and leading at the edge of our abilities. I love how unforced our rhythm as a team is. Bryan, Lindi, Diane, Eric, Ryan, and Trent let's keep climbing!

Mike, thanks for being an incredible neighbor. Your support and love play such an important part of the last 5 years. Countless Saturdays around the fire pit, Madden football games, and needing to borrow your truck where identity, mission, community first struck me leave no doubt at the gift of your friendship.

For those that gave so much of their time to help me see in the midst of a great darkness thank you. Steve, Larry, and Rich your consistency helped me stabilize.

When those words were journaled in 2006, Keith you were there. Thank you friend. I'll never forget.

For those that generously gave to help us out financially, like I always say, "You will always share in this!"

For those who helped edit the early copies of this manuscript and gave time to the dissertation research, thank you! Amanda, Wray, Casey, Matt, Eric B, Jess, Kevin, Charlie, Josh, Eric R, Christopher, John, Cindy, Ron, Karen, Kevin, Tiffany, Tracy, Keith, Karrie, Fred, David, Billy, I appreciate it.

SIGHT/SHIFT EVENTS

SightShift events are designed for churches, ministries and businesses to live and lead for a solid core.

We've watched these transform organizations, leadership teams and volunteers. Options for event speaking, day long training or multiple-day retreats are available.

Learn more...

SIGHTSHIFT.COM/EVENTS

MARRIAGE/SHIFT

SightShift for couples. MarriageShift includes resources, seminars and training for married couples.

Experiencing security in Jesus, gain clarity in your role as a spouse and foster a life-giving, intimate relationship.

Find out more…

MARRIAGESHIFT.COM

CHAMPION/SHIFT

ChampionShift exists to spread the SightShift message in the arena of athletics, helping athletes learn who they are apart from their performance.

ChampionShift is currently in beta.

Sign up for updates....

ChampionShift.com

ABOUT CHRIS MCALISTER

Chris has pastored and served in churches small and large for over fifteen years. He is pastor of Discovery Church in Columbus, Ohio. He is an adjunct professor at Capital University and he is the CEO of the parent company of SightShift. Leading staff, teams, and individuals Chris helps leaders see how their internal world drives their external leadership. Through SightShift events Chris helps people discover freedom from comparison and fear. Chris is focused on helping others learn to experience a secure identity which will overflow into a clear mission and build healthy community.

Married to Brandi for 13 years and raising 3 daughters he knows the pressures, demands, and joys of family life.

ABOUT BRET BURCHARD

After college, Bret entered the real world chasing a big dream. He immediately secured three part-time jobs and earned a master's degree while living in the back of a barber shop. A basketball junkie, Bret is now the assistant video coordinator for the Phoenix Suns (NBA).

In October 2011, Bret began digesting the SightShift message through Chris' website and applying the truths of SightShift to his own life. One year later, Bret flew to Ohio for the immersive experience of a SightShift retreat. Just a few months later, inspired to help build a movement, Bret joined Chris on his climb to complete this book.

Bret's passion is to spread the SightShift message in the athletics arena through ChampionShift, helping athletes separate who they are from their performance in competition.

Made in the USA
San Bernardino, CA
21 March 2014